blue
rider
press

TRESPASSING ACROSS AMERICA

ALSO BY KEN ILGUNAS

Walden on Wheels:
On the Open Road from Debt to Freedom

TRESPASSING
ACROSS AMERICA

One Man's Epic, Never-Done-Before

(and Sort of Illegal) Hike

across the Heartland

←→

KEN ILGUNAS

BLUE RIDER PRESS

NEW YORK

blue
rider
press

An imprint of Penguin Random House LLC
375 Hudson Street
New York, New York 10014

ISBN 9780399175480

Printed in the United States of America
1   3   5   7   9   10   8   6   4   2

BOOK DESIGN BY AMANDA DEWEY
FRONTMATTER MAP BY MEIGHAN CAVANAUGH

Penguin is committed to publishing works of quality and integrity.
In that spirit, we are proud to offer this book to our readers; however,
the story, the experiences, and the words are the author's alone.

Ten percent of author royalties will be donated to the Prairie Plains Resource Institute, an educational land trust based in Aurora, Nebraska, dedicated to the preservation, restoration, and stewardship of native prairies, and to their use for educational purposes.

Wanderer, your footsteps are
the road, and nothing more;
wanderer, there is no road,
the road is made by walking.

→ Antonio Machado

1.

Escape from Prudhoe Bay

DEADHORSE, ALASKA

Fall 2011

←→

I can say this from experience: There's nothing like washing spoon after spoon in the middle of the night in a silent kitchen at a working camp three hundred miles north of the Arctic Circle that makes you think about the direction your life is headed in.

A year before I threw on a backpack and set off on a hike across North America, I found myself driving a mud-caked van full of bed linens to a working camp in Alaska called Deadhorse, where I was to assume the position of camp dishwasher.

It was a 250-mile ride up the gravel and dirt Dalton Highway that links the interior of the state to the Prudhoe Bay oil fields along the Arctic Ocean coast. It was late and dark, yet the storm clouds zipping from one end of the sky to the other still held within them a curious pink-red hue. Between the time lapse–like passage of the clouds and the deathly still tundra plain (where the wind has no trees to shake or leaves to scatter), I felt as if I were entering some disturbing, un-worldly, goat-headed netherworld.

"This place is just weird," said Liam, a cook in the passenger seat, looking up at the clouds.

"I was thinking the same thing," I said.

Deadhorse houses about three thousand oil-field laborers who live at the work camp for a month at a time before they fly back to wher-ever's home for a week or two. In Deadhorse, there are no churches, schools, families, or anything that would make it resemble a normal American town. It is a cold, lifeless, cheerless (and nearly femaleless) place where nobody in his right mind would ever want to live—an assertion that would insult no one, as it is held most ardently by those who call themselves permanent residents.

I pulled into the Deadhorse Camp parking lot and carefully stepped out into fifty-mile-per-hour winds, placing my feet into the mud-gravel ground with all of my weight for fear that my armful of linens and I would capsize with the next heavy gust.

How I found myself in Deadhorse is worth a story of its own, but suffice it to say, I was desperate and needed money. I'd moved up to Alaska with the intention of turning a series of blog essays (from my web site, regrettably named "The Spartan Student") into a book about a few years of my life during which I lived in a van so that I could afford grad school. But after a series of disappointments, I had to set my sights on the much more practical task of eking out a living.

Deadhorse Camp is a steely rectangular Halliburton housing unit that runs entirely on diesel fuel. I worked alongside four coworkers all my age, cooking and cleaning for about fifty oil-field workers who stayed at our camp. Oddly enough, three of us had college degrees in English—a degree that clearly did nothing to prepare us for the duties of succeeding in the professional world but did, however, empower us to have impassioned forty-five-minute conversations about whether the film *Scream* does or does not fit within the horror genre.

I was given one side of a red-and-white outdoor Travco trailer that was outfitted with giant skis so it could be dragged over the ice in winter. The manager encouragingly referred to it as my "writing studio," but the desk, which had been glued to the wall decades before, fell off the moment I placed my laptop on it.

Coworkers shared the communal shower with the tourists and pipeline workers. Because, as we were told, water cost thirty-five cents a gallon, it was no surprise that the water flowed from the shower nozzle at an exasperating dribble. The water pressure being so slight, I had to stand directly beneath it. Whenever I turned to wash a different part of my body, I'd accidentally nudge the hot-cold dial, which was hypersensitive, so much so that a millimeter adjustment to the left or right would send either a boiling, skin-melting trickle onto my shoulders or a polar, heart-stopping slush.

I didn't mind my accommodations at all. In fact, I was plenty amused with the novelty of the camp and its eccentric drabness, but the work—the work!—was depressing. I'd come into the kitchen at six p.m. (the "dish shift") and scrub the bottoms of burned soup pots, dip my hand into sink drains to pluck out handfuls of slippery vegetables, and cram heavy black industrial trash bags into polar bear–proof Dumpsters. I'd set up the salad bar, slice the bread, arrange the dessert rack, fold used cardboard, and clean up the kitchen for the morning cook. There once was a time when I was a student, a park ranger, an adventurer. And now look at me. *Dishwasher.*

. . .

"I t sounds like your inner Odysseus is lost at sea," said Liam, Deadhorse's thirty-year-old prize chef. I'd just let out a sigh for the third time in an hour while trying to use a wire brush to scrub dried specks of mashed potato off the rim of a large metal stirring bowl.

Oh, Liam. How I liked Liam! Every evening we'd work alongside each other. He'd cook, I'd clean, and we'd talk. Our conversations were the only thing I looked forward to. Liam was a few years older than I was. He was extremely well-read and the sort of person who knows all the names of Homer's Greek characters and who could apply his erudition to everyday issues, like the way he assigned some of the few female Deadhorse oil-field laborers with personality-revealing names such as "Circe" and "Calypso." Liam was one of those rare people you come across in life who you want to stuff into a sack and carry with you wherever you go.

My Deadhorse stay was supposed to last only a couple of weeks, but it would turn into a couple of months. Over the course of the summer, I'd gone from the glorified title of writer-in-residence, to tour guide, to dishwasher, as if I were on some cruel, Scrooge-like, time-traveling tour, visiting my jobs of yesteryear, each demanding less skill and responsibility than the last.

I cursed more. I told crass, tasteless jokes. I wore smelly, stained, soup-splattered shirts. I spent my nights drinking Pabst and watching TV series after TV series, and the beginnings of a paunch steadily strained the elastic in my black kitchen pants. I knew things were going from pathetic to thinking, *Maybe Cymbalta is right for me?* when I dropped a tray of turkey lunch meat onto the floor, and instead of cursing, I just stared at the meat sprawled across the linoleum in deadly silence.

"We need to get out," Liam said. "We need to see the ocean."

Our plan was to walk five miles to the Sagavanirktok (or Sag) River and paddle north three miles to the Arctic Ocean in lightweight inflatable kayaks called packrafts. We'd then paddle west for a few miles along the coast before heading back to Deadhorse, where we needed to be back in time for our kitchen shifts the next morning.

We put on dry suits, strapped light backpacks around our shoulders, and hiked out over the flat, firm, easy-on-the-feet tundra. The fall foliage was colored with squash yellows, apple reds, and pumpkin oranges. Most of the birds had migrated south, but there were vestiges of summer swarms of flying life: snowy owls, loons, floating gulls, flocks of geese, and a clatter of ravens. Off to the north—through Liam's binoculars—we saw a golden eagle on the ground flapping its wings at a ghost-white arctic fox that was obnoxiously running laps around it.

We inflated the packrafts and let the Sag—swift and powerful at these northern latitudes—carry us to the Arctic Ocean. The ocean, though, wasn't a mere couple of miles away as Liam thought it was. Behind every bend in the river, we expected to see the chilly gray expanse of the ocean, but the river continued to meander northward with no end in sight.

Our leisurely paddle downriver was brought to a halt when we caught sight of something big and white and round. Liam and I pulled over to the bank instinctively.

"Do you see that?" I asked.

He took out his binoculars.

"I don't know what it is, but it's big and it's moving," Liam said nervously.

We were unarmed except for a canister of bear spray, and we had no strategy for dealing with a polar bear except to (1) wait for it to get within twenty feet so we could drizzle it with a puff of cayenne or (2) drop everything and hopelessly scamper across the empty tundra, which, with each passing second, appeared to be the far more sensible option.

I frantically deflated my raft and sloppily strapped it to the outside of my pack with frozen hands covered in wet sand. The polar bear continued its swim toward us, my heart leaping every time I looked up and saw that it was getting closer. It was only a matter of seconds before we would have to drop everything and enthusiastically commit to our coldly Darwinian "whoever's fastest wins" option number two, but the bear turned out to be nothing more than a drifting seagull leisurely floating down the Sag. (One's depth perception, we learned, cannot be trusted on this flat, lunar, North Slope landscape.)

Okay, no polar bear, thank God, but we had other problems to deal with. For one, because of the rushed, slapdash nature of our adventure, we didn't think to bring any sleeping bags or tents. And because we were so far north and well past the northern tree line, there was no wood to start a fire. And after looking at my GPS, I saw that we had a twelve-mile hike back to Deadhorse, which would actually be more like fifteen when you factor in all the ponds, lakes, and tundra bog we'd have to walk around. And our biggest problem: We would have to walk through the vigilantly monitored, hyper-secure Prudhoe Bay oil field—the largest oil field in North America that, before drilling started in 1977, held twenty-five billion barrels of oil. Hiking through the oil field is strictly prohibited, and while we had no desire to break the law, there was no way we could get around Prudhoe Bay. We'd have to sneak through. We'd have to trespass.

We had walked a mile southwest, or what we thought was southwest, and when I looked down and picked up my pack, which I'd set down a moment before, I wasn't sure which direction we'd come from and which direction we were supposed to head toward. I did a 360. And then another 360. I was spinning.

The land around us was perfectly flat. The sky was an overcast gray. Everything, up and down, left and right, looked exactly the same. I frantically spun and spun and spun, seeking a hill, a distant building, or a blotch of sunshine behind the clouds that might bring some sense to this senselessly unvarying plains landscape. But there was nothing. I pulled out my GPS, and it gave a different directional reading each time I looked at it. Twisting in circles, my compass seemed to be just as disoriented as I was. The plains, which I'd thought to be the epitome of monotony and tranquility, turned out to be as mysterious and menacing as the core of a smoldering volcano.

Sit down, Ken, I told myself. *Calm down.*

But in addition to panic, I felt something else: the jolt of a raw encounter with an unforgiving wilderness, the exuberance of having a firsthand experience with the world, a wild gush of emotions that made me feel, though scared and panicky, overflowing with life.

I sat down and made myself eat a sandwich. My compass needle ceased its spinning, and I was finally able to locate the bland southwesterly direction we needed to head toward.

Hours passed. Night replaced day and a frosty mist clung to my facial hair. On the edge of a lake in front of us stood a giant bull caribou bearing a curled crown of antlers that were orbited by two batlike short-eared owls, both of which—after the caribou had regally trotted off and disappeared into the fog—came to inspect us, hovering silently above our heads like kites.

The distant horizon was speckled with the lights of oil camps and roadway lamps. In front of us was one such oil camp, a small metallic facility with about a dozen outdoor lights. We were all whispers now, wary of being caught and having to deal with the possibility of an interrogation, a fine for trespassing, or something worse. It was close to midnight, so we thought we could slip by undetected. As we neared the building, we saw some humanlike movement. A spotlight clicked on. Whoever was manning the light drew figure eights onto the tundra until he trained the spotlight directly on us.

"We're screwed," I whispered.

"Just stay still," Liam said. "If they come near, just lie on the ground."

"What? I don't know, man. Maybe it would be better if we just gave in if they've already caught us."

I was equal parts disturbed by and admiring of Liam's composure. How was he not nervous? We stood still for minutes—two mannequins frozen in midstride whispering out of the corners of our mouths—until we decided that the guy with the spotlight was probably too far away to see us. We started hiking again, lengthening our strides and adding an alarmed briskness to our gaits. We reached an industrial road and placed our footsteps in sync with each other's to reduce the volume of our boots' crunch over the gravel. We ducked under a pipeline and continued on.

There were lights everywhere in all directions. White lights, orange lights, red lights, blinking lights, the lights of trucks prowling from facility to facility. They knew we were out there. Because of the depth perception problem, we couldn't tell which lights were close and which were far away. The buzz of machines was everywhere: beeps, honks, and whirring engines that had us swiveling our heads every few moments.

Looking over the facilities, I thought that there was something disturbing about this place, this barren coastal plain. I'd felt it ever since I'd come up here and more so now that I was walking through the oil fields. The place made me think of the film *Black Narcissus*, set in the Himalayas in an old palace that a few well-meaning nuns were trying in vain to transform into a school. The wind from the mountains drove the nuns mad. It never stopped. It moved into their rooms, invading, molesting, reminding them, like a ghost, that this place is and always will be a place of kings and queens, jewels and perfumes, self-indulgence and debauchery, and that you can either accept that or die trying to change it.

That's how I felt about Deadhorse. That we shouldn't be there. That this place was meant to be still and silent, unbothered and undeveloped. The giant drills, the mud-spattered trucks, the rusty oil barrels, the big diesel-run complex. It bore a special brand of ugliness— the ugliness of a place existing in complete disharmony with its surroundings. The oil was finite and Deadhorse was temporary. We'll make a mess of the area for a few decades, then leave the corrugated mess to the cold and wind forever after. And we are not real inhabitants—just suckerfish along for the ride, desperately clinging to the belly of the great oil-filled beast.

The Inuit, who once lived along these shores, built homes from the earth, kayaks from skins, clothes from fur. They lived and died here for thousands of years, leaving not the slightest blemish on the land. Surely they didn't view the coastal plain the way the oilman does. Here, the Inuit's eye was probably drawn to caribou browsing amid a near-endless field of ripe cotton grass, the ecstatic leap of an ocean fish, the braided sinew of a perfectly crafted bow. I'm guessing, but everything they saw must have glistered brightly with the beauty of sustainability, which is the same thing as the beauty of belonging: They knew that this place was their home and would always be their home, that their livelihoods were in harmony with the land—a sensation unknown to most all of us. We, on the other hand, don't belong up here. At least not in this way. A place like this could drive a man mad.

Atop a pingo—a mound of earth-covered ice—the silhouette of an arctic fox appeared. It tilted its head back and unleashed a cackling howl. I strode past it, keeping an eye on it, worried that its screams would draw the eyes of prowling oilmen. When I looked forward, I saw Liam pumping his arms, running as fast as he could over land he couldn't see beneath him. I mimicked Liam's sprint until I got to where he was and dived behind another pingo.

"Why are we running?" I whispered between breaths.

"There's a truck following us with a spotlight," he said. "You didn't see it?"

We heard the growl of the truck just behind the pingo, slowly prowling past while sweeping the spotlight over the land.

This is it, I thought. *All they have to do is get out and look over this pingo, and we're caught.*

In truth, if we were caught, we probably wouldn't have received more than a slap on the wrist, but without thinking about it, I suppose we wanted to be scared, nervous, and panicky as we trespassed across forbidden lands. To those sound in spirit, this trip would likely have been considered unpleasant, but for those in existential despair, such unpleasantness can function as a restorative distraction, a resuscitating shock, a defibrillator charge to the soul.

The oilmen never spotted us, and we continued on through night and fog, around lakes, and across the other waist-high branch of the Sag until we staggered into Deadhorse Camp.

The trip was a disaster, but I thought: *What would I do to have the life of the hiker?!* It was more than just a form of escape. On a hike, the days pass with the wind, the sun, the stars; movement is powered by a belly of food and water, not a noxious tankful of fossil fuels. On a hike, you're less a job title and more a human being. Our commute, our shift, our shows: How quickly does the routine—masquerading as life—block from our view the grand vistas of possibility. A periodic hike not only stretches the limbs but also reminds us: Wow, there's a big old world out there.

"This is the best experience I've had in a long time," said Liam.

"I know," I said. "Me, too."

Invigorated by our hike, we found the tone of our kitchen conversations turning from friendly intellectual heart-to-hearts to something far more fanatical. As the purposeless are wont to do, Liam and I continued to fantasize about grandeur, high adventure, true purpose. (At this moment, kitchen crews everywhere are plotting to take over the world.) Disgusted with what the oil industry had turned the Arctic coast into, we discussed putting a team of radical environmentalists together to commit acts of environmental terrorism. Liam would be the cook, I would be the letter-to-the-editor guy, and Liam "knew a guy" who might know a thing or two about explosives. These discussions would always begin in a spirit of whimsical and good-humored facetiousness, but would, by the end, take on an unsettling seriousness as we delved into the particulars: *So do you or do you not know a guy?*

The Keystone XL Pipeline had become a hot topic during our nightly discussions. We'd read that protestors were performing acts of civil disobedience to oppose the pipeline that, if approved, would transport 830,000 barrels of tar-sands oil every day across the continent and help expand the already expansive tar sands of northern Alberta.

There was something about being up in Deadhorse that made the idea of the 1,700-mile pipeline particularly upsetting. Here we were at ground zero of American oil development. We saw the industrial squalor, the depraved lifestyles, the sad, empty eyes of the workers. We felt the emptiness within ourselves. This place was an Ayn Rand wasteland, the epitome of our country's wrongheaded conception of "progress." The thought of creating more such places, more such jobs, and more such planet-warming greenhouse gases defied, in our eyes, all the tenets of good sense and reason.

We wondered: If we totally buy into the evidence and civilization-ending projections of global warming, what is our duty as citizens of this earth? Is donating to the Sierra Club enough? Is our responsibility fulfilled if we vote for the right politician and bike to work on sunny days? Or is something more required? Physical action? Violence? Terrorism? If the planet is, in fact, being slowly strangled to death, isn't it our duty to do everything in our power to stop the perpetrators? What's the most that one person can do?

"What if we hike the Keystone XL?" Liam asked out of the blue.

"You mean across country? Across private property? Across the whole continent?" I asked.

"Yeah," he said. "Just like we did in Prudhoe Bay."

Liam's idea was crazy but not an "I hope I won't have to find a way to get accepted into a gang in federal prison for being a terrorist" kind of crazy. I felt a shock—a ground-trembling lightning bolt that coursed through me, leaving in its aftermath a flurry of jitters that bordered on the erotic. Some deep, inner part of me recognized the brilliance of Liam's idea with a startling immediacy. I hadn't begun to consciously rationalize why, but some farseeing part of me knew then and there that I was going to—no, *had to*—hike the Keystone XL.

Everything began to make sense. Being in Deadhorse. The nighttime hike out of Prudhoe Bay. This crazy period of my life could only end with a crazy conclusion. I dropped the mixing bowl into the sink, looked at Liam, and said—with what must have been almost frightening excitement—"We must!"

2.

Preparation

The Keystone XL, though not yet built nor even approved, had become, I thought, the perfect symbol of the twenty-first century. It was a war zone where environmentalists were pitted against industry. It was where hopes for our future clashed with habits of our past. It was the first time that the construction of a large-scale energy project had faced a serious challenge from ordinary citizens out of concern for climate change. The fight over the pipeline would be a historically significant event whether or not it was ever built.

So even though the XL's path would lead me over the Great Plains, the "flyover" states, and what I frankly saw as the middle of nowhere, with the fate of a warming world at stake, I thought of the XL as the center of the universe—and I wanted to be there to learn everything I could about it.

Who better to walk across North America than I? I thought. I considered myself an adventurer, having hitchhiked eight thousand miles across North America over the past few years. But, truth be told, I was more a penniless and drifting tramp than a full-fledged and sponsored adventurer. Hitchhiking, anyway, is a lazy man's adventure, requiring only patience, the ability to endure hours of drivers' monologues, and a lot of sitting. I could boast of canoeing one thousand miles across Ontario, Canada, but that trip required more arms than legs and, again, an inadvisable amount of sitting. I'd also been a backcountry ranger up in the Gates of the Arctic National Park, a job that actually required that I did more than sit, but our patrols never lasted for more than a week at a time.

I'd done all those things years ago. Since then, I'd been a student—a designation that required I sit for hours, days, months(!) on end. My ass, once a sturdy hockey-player's hillock of meat and muscle, had, over the years, turned into a pale downward-leaning sack of fat, a drooping Salvador Dali clock that looked all the more pathetic on the body of an otherwise healthy twentysomething.

Come to think of it, maybe I wasn't suited for the task, as I had neither the training, nor the body, nor the experience to embark on a five-month-long hike across the New World. But what I could say for myself was that I had the gusto to think I could actually do it, the desire to test my physical limits, and, most of all, the aching need to once and for all get off my ass and hike.

O ver the next year, after my Keystone XL epiphany, I had a surprising string of successes. I hitchhiked out of Deadhorse, restarted work on my book about living in a van, got a book deal, pulled myself out of my financial quagmire, kicked the mice out of my van in North Carolina, and moved into my best friend Josh's basement in Denver, Colorado, where I began to plan my trip.

Liam and I had stayed in touch all that time to discuss trip logistics. At first, the expedition, along with most of my other ideas, could have been listed under the category of "Things I fantasize about doing, and probably won't (but are fun to think about doing anyway)."

We had monthly phone conversations about the trip. It was clear that I was far more excited about the expedition than he was, but by the end of each conversation, he seemed to be reenergized and rededicated. I'd begun to wonder, though, if Liam had the frame of mind necessary to commit to such a long journey. For one thing, he began to question if it would be better to wait another year so we could properly "prepare and save up enough money." More unsettling was his suggestion that we "don't have to do the whole thing" and that we could "hike for a bit, take some months off, and start again whenever we wanted to." Such suggestions were hardly unreasonable, but I'd read enough books on real-life journeys to appreciate how "reasonableness" isn't always a good trait for someone who's about to do something ultimately unreasonable.

Still, I so wanted Liam to come. I knew that he'd be the perfect traveling companion. He was kind, intelligent, a great cook, and I knew from our Prudhoe Bay hike that Liam had an on-the-ground ballsiness that I wanted to have but didn't, and that this ballsiness was something we'd likely need on a journey where we'd have to trespass over private property, steal water from farms, and probably piss off the oil industry. I pictured the two of us trudging across the lonely wide-open prairie like Sam and Frodo on a long, perilous journey.

We'd take care of each other, lift each other up when we were down, and, perhaps, like the Hobbits in moments of utter hopelessness, hold hands in that tender, brotherly, pre-twentieth-century, and not-at-all-gay way. I imagined us on a journey of high adventure: escaping gunfire, taking cover from tornados, and maybe whispering in a moment of life-or-death suspense, with a hushed tone of poised determination: *"Run."*

I wanted ours to be a gritty journey. America's great trails, like the Appalachian Trail and Pacific Crest Trail, span more than two thousand miles and are by no means easy (and anyone who finishes one of them is deserving of our respect as someone who is certifiably *badass*), but to me, these trails hardly seemed adventurous. Typically, these megatrails are well marked, come with guidebooks, have three-walled shelters and signs pointing to water sources. And, of course, they're *trails*, meaning that someone else has taken the time to blaze and maintain them so thousands of people can walk them. Consequently, the people and animals around these trails are so used to seeing hikers that opportunities for unique encounters and mutual curiosity are rare. And I thought that these trails were hardly representative of America: They divert around towns, industry, poverty, and in so doing, divert around reality. They keep their walkers on a thin and protected corridor of wilderness on a continent that is getting increasingly less wild.

I didn't want to trespass across the continent purely to take pictures of pretty landscapes or even to see those last vestiges of a once-wild continent (though I hoped to do at least a bit of each). More than anything, I wanted to get closer to understanding the world for what it is, and if that meant I'd feel more revulsion than admiration, then so be it. I was in it for the knowledge, the insight, the shock. Beauty, for the true traveler, is merely a bonus.

Plus, I knew that walking the XL across the Great Plains—a route that no one had ever taken before—would give me a chance to feel something closer to what Lewis and Clark had felt two hundred years before: the thrill of not knowing what's behind the next hill, who I'd meet, what would attack me, or how I'd react. I wanted the life of the explorer, the adventurer, so that I would come to thank the cosmos for making the planet a sphere, keeping its explorers in a state of wonder for what awaits them beyond the earth's ever-changing, never-ending curve.

I t was May, just a couple of months before the beginning of our trip, when Liam suddenly remembered that he was still banned from Canada for an undisclosed offense he'd committed in that country years ago during what he referred to as his "wayward youth."

I suggested that we figure out a way to sneak him across the border so we could get to northern Alberta (our starting point), but he—in a disappointing and uncharacteristic exhibition of prudence—decided to drop out of the expedition altogether.

The loss of Liam was devastating, and reimagining the trip as a solo undertaking wasn't going to be easy. The thought of figuring out the exact route of the Keystone XL, of somehow creating maps for the trip, of packing boxes of food to be shipped to towns along my path, of outfitting myself with gear, of somehow getting up to Alberta, and of walking it all by myself seemed like such a daunting, life-consuming job that it was almost enough to make me drop out, too.

For weeks I told my friends that I was still going on the hike, but I was trying to get them to believe something I myself did not. In a moment of self-doubt-induced self-examination, I asked myself, *Am I the sort of person who leaves everything behind and goes on a grand, uncertain, never-done-before adventure?* My answer wasn't quite a yes, but it was good enough: *Why not?*

I went online and spent $250 on mapping software. Cheapskate that I am, the investment of money turned out to be a momentous turning point when "crazy idea" turned into "actual plan." Now that money was invested, I was invested. This was the point of no return.

Between the software and some maps of the XL on the U.S. government's web site, I was able to figure out my route and print out about fifty topographic maps, which took me a little more than a week.

Once I figured out my route, I focused on how I was going to feed myself. Like most thru-hikers who hike the lengths of major American trails, I figured the most efficient way to hike and feed myself would be to package boxes of food, and have a friend mail those boxes to post offices along my route, where I could pick them up.

I figured I'd need about 4,000 calories a day, so I made a daily meal plan, then bought a Sam's Club membership and purchased $1,000 worth of food: 6.5 pounds of powdered mashed potatoes, 7 pounds of dehydrated whole milk, 17 pounds of trail mix, 2 pounds of instant refried beans, 15 canisters of Parmesan cheese, 228 candy bars (Snickers, 3 Musketeers, Mounds, Nestlé Crunch, Hershey's, Hershey's Cookies 'n' Creme), 300 energy bars, 15 cans of Pringles, 216 Pop-Tarts, and $100 worth of granola.

Daily meal plan	Ounces	Calories
Breakfast: Granola/whole milk	7 (4.5 cereal/2.5 milk)	840 calories
Snack 1: CLIF Bar	2.4	240 calories
Snack 2: CLIF/pemmican bar	2.4/3.75	240/210 calories
Snack 3: Pemmican bar	3.75	210 calories
Snack 4: Trail mix	3	450 calories
Snack 5: Pringles	1/3 of a can (2 oz.)	300 calories
Snack 6: Chocolate bar	2.1	280 calories
Snack 7: Chocolate bar	2.1	280 calories
Snack 8: Pop-Tart	1.8	205 calories
Dinner	6.3	900 calories
Total	2 lbs., 1 oz.	3,945 calories

After buying and packaging all of my food, I went on a gear spending spree with my book-deal money, buying a rain suit, a lightweight
sleeping bag, a sixty-five-liter backpack, a set of thermal underwear,
a light synthetic jacket, and a baseball hat. I bought a canister of bear
spray and a jackknife for protection, a pair of trekking poles, a one-
and-a-half-pound tarp tent, a foam sleeping pad, and countless small
essentials such as sunscreen, lip balm, chlorine dioxide water-treatment
drops, three collapsible water bottles, med kit, wristwatch, match-
books, headlamp, sewing needle and thread, compass, notepad and
pens, toothbrush, toothpaste, and floss. I packed one pot and made a
stove out of an empty cat-food can into which I'd pour a couple of
ounces of alcohol. Upon igniting the alcohol, it would bring my water
in the pot to a boil within a couple of minutes. I wanted to be able to
blog about my trip, so I bought an iPad and a monthly cellular-data

subscription. I added a small camera, cell phone, passport, and porta-ble solar charger.

I shoved it all in my pack, along with five days' worth of food, and weighed it: a troubling forty-five pounds that I'd have to carry for the next several months.

Everything was coming together. I had my food and my gear. Josh agreed to mail me packages to post offices along my route. I'd kept up on my training regimen, jogging five miles a day to get my legs in hiking shape. It was looking like I'd be able to start my trip in July as planned, which meant, if I walked from north to south, I'd be hiking through warm weather for the length of my trip, catching the "latitu-dinal sweet spot" where the temperature would be nice and mild across all the states and provinces I'd walk. I'd be in Alberta in a not-so-hot July and Texas in a not-so-cold December.

Book-editing duties, however, took longer than expected, delay-ing my departure by weeks. Plus, Josh had announced that he was getting married in late August, and he wanted me to be his best man. I postponed the trip for another month.

Finally freed of work and social obligations, I prepared to leave, but I tripped when scurrying down Josh's basement stairs. My left little toe got caught on the edge of a step. I heard an awful snap, hob-bled to my room, fell onto the inflatable mattress, broke out in a cold sweat, and silently hoped that I hadn't broken a major bone in my foot. Luckily, it was only my little toe, which instantly became swol-len and turned pink.

I'd never tripped down stairs or broken a toe in my life, but I hap-pen to do so just days before I was to set off on a hiking expedition? I wondered if my subconscious—which perhaps had grave misgivings about the expedition—was taking drastic measures by secretly laying booby traps and sacrificing negligible body parts for my own good. Might I have been hurting myself purposefully? Were two parts of my psyche waging war against each other without my even knowing it?

I needed to give the toe at least another week and a half to heal, which guaranteed that my expedition would no longer be in the summer and fall, but in the fall and winter.

I had more than enough excuses not to go and I wasn't looking for any more, so I resolved not to research my route too closely. I knew I was better off not knowing about unfordable rivers, impenetrable forests, or prairie cougars. Naïveté, though a shortcoming in most any other situation, is a prerequisite to adventure. (Stupidity can be an outright asset.) But now that I could do nothing but lounge around in my underwear and recuperate, I thought that I should perhaps use some of my downtime constructively and figure out exactly what those swampy symbols were on my maps that were in the middle of my route for the first three hundred miles.

But who does one call for advice on how to illegally follow a controversial pipeline? I called a Canadian oil company's offices in northern Alberta but quickly slammed the phone down when I was put on a line with a human. I did a little Googling and found the phone number of a hunting guide in Alberta who led tours on some of the rivers I'd have to cross.

"You'll probably get thrown in jail," he said, pointing out that the first leg of my journey, from Fort McMurray to Hardisty, Alberta, led me right through the middle of a military zone. "And you're going to be chin-high in muskeg. Where you're going, they usually take amphibious vehicles."

"I'm sure I'm going to sound stupid asking this, but what's muskeg?"

"It's swamp," he said. "It's all swamp and forest up here."

I could tell from this guy's tone that he wasn't trying to scare me or put on an air of expertise and machismo. He was informative, serene, and calm, which made what he had to say all the more alarming.

I now had serious questions about my route, the temperature and weather, and my toe, which had turned a deep shade of purple. I had no partner, no experience with thru-hikes; and I didn't even know how I was going to get to Canada. The trip had gone from being the serious undertaking of a wannabe adventurer to a laugh-out-loud farce.

As I inched closer to embarking on my hike—and when it seemed that this might be one of the few things I actually follow through with—the conversations with my mother became grimmer than usual, in which she'd call to hysterically inform me about my impending death.

"You're going to get shot for walking on someone else's property," she'd say. "Yeah, keep laughing. You'll see."

Perhaps she was right to be concerned. To take off to northern lands on the eve of winter with a purple toe and no trail to follow or guidebook to consult would be, to most rational thinkers, insane. Yet since everything about the tar sands and the XL and America's contempt for the reality of climate change struck me as insane, too, I thought it would be fitting to embrace this spirit of insanity, throw all caution to the wind, and embark on my adventure anyway.

The thought of quitting before starting flitted through my mind, but it seemed as if prudence and good judgment were losing out to my philosophy of "Fuck it, I'm going anyway."

. . .

A h, the preadventure jitters! If only we were kept awake every night by the delirious anticipation of tomorrow!

On my last night in Denver, Josh and his wife made me a going-away dinner of chicken, sweet-potato fries, salad, and peach pie. Afterward, while watching the Bears-Packers game on TV in his basement, we heard what sounded like someone frantically banging on the front door upstairs. The sound was actually about a half-dozen gunshots from the street just in front of the house. (Josh lives in a semi-sketchy area in inner-city Denver, and the occurrence of a drive-by wasn't entirely out of the ordinary.)

In the morning, I looked to see if there was any damage done to my van, which was parked in the street. I was glad to see that it had gone unscathed while the station wagon next to it was pocked with six bullet holes. I took this as a good omen on the day I'd begin my trip—a trip on which I'd constantly have to escape bad luck (and possibly gunfire).

I hopped on a bus that would take me as far north as Fort Collins, Colorado. There were no more northward buses from there, and I didn't know exactly how I was going to travel the 1,500 miles north, but none of that mattered because the moment I hobbled with my sore toe out onto the I-25 thruway ramp—though far from home, my things, and my friends—I felt like the freest, happiest person on Earth.

I'm actually doing this, aren't I? I asked myself, elated.

I'm actually doing this, I said to myself, more glumly.

What the hell am I doing? I thought, looking despairingly back toward Denver.

3.

The Hitchhike

September 2012

← →

A part from a moment or two of cold feet, I walked toward the busy I-25 in a flurry of ecstasy that began in my belly, coursed up the length of my spine, and erupted out of my mouth in wild cackles of exultation that I tried to hide from passing drivers for fear that they'd think I was crazy.

I was aglow, thankful for life, this life, with which, it was so apparent right then, I could do anything I fancied. I was living! Fully and unabashedly, wholly and unfettered! Life! It's all mine.

The beginning of an adventure . . . Yes, there will be misery and, yes, I will be miserable, but right now, at the beginning, there are only sunny skies and grand visions of what my newly adventurous future holds. There won't be any more schedules. No more bosses. No more dishes, no more bills. I am on the open road carrying only a backpack full of gear and a far-fetched idea: to get to Alberta and then walk every step of the way south to Texas. Whatever trials and triumphs that lie ahead are unknown. What will I see? Whom will I meet? Who will I be by the time I reach the end?

I was heading north toward the deep, dark, green forests of northern Alberta where, before I could commence my hike, I needed to see the tar sands—the source of the oil that would travel through the Keystone XL.

Where would I get my water from? How would landowners react to my trespassing over their property? How was I going to deal with all the animals—especially the cows? I'd have to walk through countless herds of them . . .

My only comfort was in knowing that I wasn't carrying some stiff, stubborn, stagnant plan but the living, breathing, heart-thumping philosophy that had worked for me so well in the past and that I believed would work for me again: *I'll figure it out.*

Much to my surprise, there was another hitchhiker on the entrance ramp standing where I'd intended to stand. He waved me over and introduced himself as Chris. He said he'd been standing there for hours. Chris was fortyish. His head was shaved bald, and he had a pair of burly, hairy, butcher's forearms. I didn't blame the drivers for passing him by; as scary as Chris looked, I probably would have, too. He told me that he'd just gotten out of jail and was headed to California to talk with his ex-girlfriend, who out of spite, apparently, cut up all of his IDs. He asked me how much money I made hitching rides, and I said, "None. I don't like to take money. Just rides." He said that begging drivers is the way he makes money and that he once left Kentucky with four hundred dollars. I gave him three candy bars and began walking up the I-25 with a cardboard sign strapped to my pack reading NORTH.

After half an hour, I was disappointed to note that my feet were already sore. While I'd jogged for weeks to train for the expedition, I hadn't accustomed myself to walking with a forty-pound backpack. The only thing that would prepare me for a long-distance hike, I realized, was a long-distance hike.

I walked on a side road that paralleled the interstate next to a cornfield where thousands of grasshoppers clumsily leaped into a jungle of sturdy green stalks and sagging, tongue-shaped leaves. An older gentleman in a white Volkswagen prowled beside me. I nodded hello. He drove off, turned around, and picked me up.

His name was Richard and he was coming from Denver, where he had attended a model train sale. He told me he was headed home to Cheyenne, Wyoming, as he handed me a napkin and a juicy plum. He talked about his Volkswagen's impressive mileage per gallon, and I casually mentioned something about how fuel-efficiency standards had recently been raised by President Obama, who, at the time, was in a dead heat in the polls with Republican presidential candidate Mitt Romney. While Richard didn't seem to have anything against the new standards, he harrumphed contemptuously at the very mention of the president's name, as if it were poison to his ears, as if it were some garlic-breathed satanic verse whispered in a schoolchild's ghostly Sanskrit. *O-ba-ma.*

Trying to address his harrumph courteously and apolitically, I asked him which of Obama's policies were not to his liking.

"All of them!" he cried, as if it were the only reasonable thing to say.

He glanced over at me suspiciously, and said, "You don't like the guy, do you?"

"I wouldn't call myself a fan," I said. "But I'm not anti-Obama."

Truth was, I went door-to-door for Obama before the 2008 election as a doe-eyed progressive, hoping he'd be the revolutionary leader who would take us from the medieval "drill-baby-drill" Cheney era into the free-thinking, the-climate's-getting-a-little-hot-so-maybe-we-should-(you-know)-do-something-about-it twenty-first century. But after four years, like many progressives, I was disillusioned with the broken promises, the galling compromises, the weak-kneed, pragmatic politics when the country needed a good, hard progressive kick to the seat of its pants.

"Well, if you say another good word about him, I'll throw you out of this car," Richard said in a joking-yet-not-really-joking sort of way, clearly dissatisfied with my response.

"I'll hold my tongue," I said obediently.

I tried to bring up his toy-train collection to move the conversation onto less hostile terrain, but something always made him think of Obama.

"He's done everything wrong!" he screeched. "Everything!"

While it was true that I, too, was disappointed, I'd like to think my disappointment was rooted in rationality. But I could tell that Richard felt something closer to hatred, which was rooted in something else entirely.

Richard was actually really nice when he wasn't talking politics, and he gave me his number in case I got stuck in Cheyenne, where he dropped me off.

"I'm sad to see you go," he said. "Give me a call if you get stuck, and I'll come pick you up."

I got a ride to Casper, Wyoming, from a National Guard JAG. We talked about his tour in Afghanistan as I looked over the Wyoming scenery—a dry, flat, brushy landscape empty except for a surprising preponderance of energy oddities: a giant two-chimney coal factory, a herd of black pump jacks pumping oil from the ground, and in the distance, the twirling arms of windmill robots. Without any roads or homes or people, these structures seemed as if they'd been dropped off by some cold, utility-minded alien race. (Unbeknownst to me, Wyoming is an energy giant. In 2012, Wyoming produced, out of all the states, the eighth most oil, the fifth most natural gas, and the most coal, more than three times second-place West Virginia).

The JAG dropped me off in Casper just before dusk. I held out my sign on an entrance ramp again but had no luck. I could see that the I-25's narrow-shouldered culvert would be dangerous to walk, so I limped along and took a side road through the low-income industrial part of town. It was getting dark, and I heard an ominous *pop* in my sock, which was a blister breaking. With each step forward, I stretched the loose skin of my broken blister. My little toe throbbed.

I pulled off my backpack, got out my medical kit, cleaned the wound with rubbing alcohol, and draped bandages over the suppurating blister while sitting on my pack on a cracked sidewalk overgrown with weeds. I hobbled down the road, nervous now. It was dark, and in this industrial sector of town, there were no trees where I could secretly set up and hide my tent. I happened upon an RV campground, but it was full, and even if it hadn't been, I didn't want to spend twenty dollars for a camping site. I continued my search until I spotted a small creek lined with big bushes next to the railroad tracks behind the campground. As long as I didn't set up my tent, I thought I might remain concealed there for the night in my sleeping bag.

The spot was far from ideal. A train clamored by every hour, and the smell of the polluted creek forced me to override my involuntary nose-based breathing patterns with an exhausting open-mouthed deliberateness. The spot's only saving grace was the incredible nighttime image of the trains that would slowly creak past my camp carrying giant windmill blades, the moonlight rolling over the smooth, steely curves and animating the march of metal into a promenade of gigantic blue whales.

In the early hours of the morning, I cooked a pot of ramen stew with my cat-food-can stove and scarfed the noodles down even though the water was too hot. I was worried about getting caught by laborers arriving to work at the nearby gravel mounds. A tramp of Native-American descent ambled north along the railroad tracks. He nodded to me, and I nodded back.

I got a lift from Blaine, an oil worker headed home to Billings, Montana. He'd just finished a twelve-hour shift after twelve straight days of work. "Long, hard, and dangerous," he described the job. "And everyone's an asshole."

He'd been working for the oil industry, grudgingly, for the past six months. His mom had cancer and couldn't work, so he took it upon himself to become the family breadwinner. He told me about all the dangerous chemicals he was daily exposed to and the high cancer rate in local towns. Recently, some of the oil had contaminated a local water supply, so large cisterns had to be set up in town, though the people still showered in the contaminated water.

He warned me about my hiking route, telling me about the wolves that had spread out across Montana from Yellowstone, not to mention the cougars, grizzly bears, freakishly strong winds, and snow that could come to Montana as soon as September, which was, unsettlingly, now.

"Do you have warm clothes?" he asked.

"Not really," I said.

The desolate Montana landscape made me shift uneasily in Blaine's passenger seat. We drove over flat land then through slightly lumpy, hilly land, shaggy with tall dry yellow-brown grass. There were no trees, no creeks, no rivers, no buildings, no people—just grass and hills and deer and black cows and nothing else. What was it going to be like walking across this? It seemed as if it would be so easy to get lost, to go thirsty, to be whisked off your feet and dropped to a gory death by an angry prairie gust. I shuddered when I remembered how disoriented I became when walking the tundra plain in northern Alaska.

Later, I got a lift from Molly and Josh, a couple in their twenties from Maine who were heading up to Glacier National Park in northern Montana on a cross-country trip to California. We camped at a national forest, and the next day they dropped me off thirty-five miles south of the Canadian border in Shelby, Montana.

I walked most of the way to the border except for a short ride with Doris, who lived in the town of Sunburst, where she owns a herd of cows. I knew I'd likely be walking through herds and herds of cows over the course of my hike, so I asked her if she thought I'd get attacked by any and what I should do if I was.

Having been raised in a suburban neighborhood, my experience with cows was, to say the least, limited. My only exposure to them had been on TV, where I'd seen them chase people in Spain, violently fling cowboys off their backs in Idaho, and horrifically gore bullfighters in some *When Animals Attack!* episode. To me, cows were not the docile bovine creatures that they were to most people but, potentially, a swarming herd of ill-tempered water buffalo that could fend off a pride of lions with their organ-rending horns and flank-to-flank formations. The very last thing I wanted was to end up on the news as the cultural spectacle of the latest person killed by an amiable animal in the once-every-few-years "Man killed by goat" story. Animals would be no small obstacle. Every year in America there are 2.8 deaths by bear, 31 by dog, 20 by cow, and the odd coyote, cougar, and mountain goat fatality. Most mammals focus in on men (71 percent of the time) and whites (91 percent of the time), making my pasty white-man butt a prime, albeit fast-moving, target. And, of course, there were people to worry about, too, with about 15,000 yearly homicides in the U.S., plus close to 1,000 hunting accidents and up to 100 annual fatalities.

"Just look them in the eye and talk to 'um manly," Doris said, about the bulls. "When they charge, just step to the side of 'um. Tire 'um out like that."

When they *charge*? Before they *hit* me? *Tire* them out? Talk to 'um *manly*?

This was not what I was hoping to hear at all! I had little faith in my ability to evade a thousand-pound hulk of spiky-headed beef and absolutely none whatsoever in my being able to maintain a masculine tone.

"But you don't have to worry about those Canadian cows," she said disdainfully. "Them are all grain fed."

Doris's advice gave me reason to believe there was some reasonableness behind my fears, but Doris, whom I spotted giving me a concerned look out of the corner of her eye, was clearly in the process of gravely bringing my intelligence into question.

"You know they're herbivores, right? That means they eat plants."

She insisted that I go back to her place for a sandwich. Doris's ex-husband, whom she'd called an "asshole" in the car, was on the couch and chose neither to get up nor look my way. When she told him she'd brought a guest home, he muttered, "Why'd you brang him here?"

Doris dropped me off on the I-15, and I stumbled on toward the border. It was dark, and no one was pulling over for me, so I walked down a steep slope next to a field where I laid out my sleeping pad and sleeping bag on a bed of grass where I was positive neither farmer nor driver would spot me. I turned on my iPad to read, but I was quickly distracted by the sky, a dark ocean lit from beneath by a wiggling world of bioluminescence. It felt as if it had been years since I'd seen the sky in all its nighttime splendor, years since I'd been on an adventure, years since I felt like I really, truly, owned my life, and all I could think of was how good it was to be alive . . .

P robably because I was so close to the Canadian border, no one picked me up the next morning. I walked the rest of the way to the border and stood in line behind a car at the inspection booth. I declared my bear spray and knife, and the agent speedily sent me into the office for further questioning. I knew what I'd planned on doing was extremely unusual and would probably be frowned upon by Canadian authorities, but I hoped my plan of lying my pants off (or until they were on fire) would do the trick and get me over the border.

"I'm going to walk across the province and write a book about the Alberta prairie," I said, with surprising aplomb, casually adding that I had my first book coming out the next year and taking care not to mention anything about the tar sands, pipelines, or my disappointment in Canada's newfound adoption of remorseless planet-destroying environmental habits. (According to the Center for Global Development's Commitment to Development Index, an annual report that ranks twenty-seven of the world's richest countries, Canada was ranked dead last in the category of "environment" from 2012–2014, in part because the tar sands place Canada among the worst greenhouse-gas-emitting countries per capita in the world.)

"Where are you going to sleep?" the official inside asked, looking curiously at my pack.

"Provincial parks whenever I can," I said.

"And motels, of course," I added, flashing her a boyish smile, as if to say, "I mean, what, do you think I'd sleep in a *farmer's field?*" (Sleeping in farmers' fields was exactly what I'd planned on doing.)

She carefully inspected my passport, noted how I was carrying a few hundred dollars in cash, and, much to my relief, let me over the border.

C anada! The boundless land of the north! The land of hockey, of boreal forest, of politeness, of universal health care! Between the unbelievably treeless, grass-waving prairie landscape and my presence in a different country, I began to feel that I was truly in foreign, exotic terrain. Yet, at the same time, it felt like a homecoming.

Twenty-nine years before, I was born in Hamilton, Ontario, to an American mom and a Scottish dad. Even though we moved to Niagara Falls, New York, when I was six, Canada would always exist in my mind as my first home, my birthplace, my maple syrup–filled womb. And as I continued to walk north on the highway, I wondered if there was something about my multinational history that had drawn me to the XL. As I did, the Keystone XL pipeline will begin in Canada and move south into America. It will be, as I am, a Canadian as well as an American product—a hybrid. I just hoped that this was the end of the metaphor since I didn't want to be refined into distillates in Texas and shipped off to China.

Now back in my native land, I took my picture with the self-timer function on my camera with my arms triumphantly raised beneath a giant WELCOME TO ALBERTA sign. I quickly got a ride with a young man attending college in Lethbridge, who told me about his travels in Japan and his education in psychology. "You didn't look like a vagrant," he said, when I asked him why he chose to pick me up.

"Thanks," I said, feeling complimented. "I prefer to think of myself more like a hitchhiker. A philosopher-tramp, maybe." Later, he took me to his parents' house so I could fill up my water bottles, and he introduced me to his sister as a "philosopher-bum."

My next ride was to Leduc, Alberta, with Jake, who worked on an oil rig near Edmonton, where he said he put in sixteen to twenty-four hours a day, oftentimes with only two to four hours of sleep between shifts.

I spent the night in my sleeping bag on the fringes of Leduc in the high grass next to an abandoned barn a short walk from the town's shopping district. The next day, I took care of a host of logistical matters. I printed out last-minute maps at a Staples, got Canadian cash from an ATM, did edits for a magazine story at the library, and tried, and ultimately failed, to figure out a way to get my defunct phone working again or get my cellular data plan working on my iPad. Since I was bringing a broken toe on a hiking trip, it seemed fitting to be bringing a bunch of completely useless communication equipment, too.

It wasn't until I was in Leduc, surrounded by people, that I realized that I cut a curious figure. Between my new backpack and fashionably stubbled facial hair (I hadn't shaved for four days), I'd unknowingly gone from ordinary person to mysterious adventurer. I found myself being ogled by female servers at the local Tim Hortons coffee shop, who muffled coquettish giggles behind cupped palms.

The next day, I took a bus to the north of Edmonton. I walked and walked, and the pain in my little toe grew more troublesome by the hour. I walked on the ball of my foot, and after that got too painful, I tried to place all the pressure on my big toe. But nothing worked. By changing how I placed my foot on the ground, I merely distributed the soreness to all sectors of my foot. I thought about standing still on the side of the road, but I had to keep walking so that I could find a good spot for cars to pull over, or better yet, an intersection where there'd be more traffic.

I tried an assortment of hitchhiker tactics: I walked with my thumb out; I walked forward with a sign strapped to my backpack; I walked backward with my thumb out. Nothing was working. I changed my sign from FORT MCMURRAY to ATHABASCA, hoping that I'd attract drivers going to this relatively nearby town rather than hoping for a driver going the whole distance. I'd hitchhiked nearly ten thousand miles across North America over the past five years, yet, in moments like these, I still managed to convince myself that despite there being no legitimate precedent to come to such a conclusion I might get stuck in this spot forever.

I was on Highway 2, which had very little traffic. The cars that did pass me were heading up the road at speeds that made me place a hand on my head to hold down my baseball cap from Frisbeeing into the woods. Finally, as evening approached, a Native American man pulled over for me and took me to Athabasca, telling me about how he and his brothers used to paddle down that road before it was a road, when it was nothing but forest and muskeg.

He dropped me off short of town. Within moments, I had another ride, with a middle-aged gentleman in a respectable-looking SUV.

"Where ya headed?" he asked.

"Atmore," I said, because that's what I had written on my sign.

"Come on in," he said. "Why are you headed to Atmore?"

"Well, I'm not headed to Atmore exactly. Sometimes it's just better to make a sign for the next closest town rather than trying to find a ride to your final destination."

"So what's your final destination?"

"The tar sands. Fort McMurray. I don't think I'll get there tonight, though. It's another three hundred kilometers."

"Well, it's your lucky day."

"Why's that?"

"'Cause that's where I'm headed."

4.

The Oilman

September 22, 2012

← →

The official name for the road that leads to the tar sands is Highway 63, but the locals have other names for it: the Highway to Hell, Hell's Highway, Suicide 63, the McMurray 500, the Highway of Death.

Highway 63 is a 150-mile, north-south, mostly two-lane road that stretches from north of Edmonton to the northern reaches of Alberta. Our destination was Fort McMurray, a flourishing boomtown of 76,000 residents, with another 39,000 living in nearby work camps.

We were driving through the boreal forest, the northern woods that stretch from Alaska all the way to Canada's east coast. From the car, it was impossible to see the ecological devastation that was supposedly going on all around us. From my seat, it just looked like a dark, dense spruce forest.

My driver, Alan, a middle-aged software engineer, was driving from Athabasca for another fourteen-day work stint. Alan was one of thousands who use the Highway to Hell every single day. It's especially bad on Tuesdays and Sundays, Alan said, because a lot of the workers ("who all drive like idiots") were finishing their work week (or work month for some) and were in a rush to get home to be with their wives or girlfriends down in Edmonton or Calgary. It's one of the deadliest roads in Canada. In 2004, the Royal Canadian Mounted Police gave out eighteen thousand tickets on just one stretch of highway, the average ticketed speed being one hundred miles per hour. Between 2002 and 2010, there were sixty-six deaths, and between 2001 and 2005, there were more than one thousand collisions and two hundred and fifty injuries.

Alan was a careful driver who never showed any emotion when a hotheaded twentysomething charged past us in his brand-new beefed-up Silverado. Curiously, Alan had installed a camera on the windshield so that when he'd eventually get into an accident his wife would be able to watch the video and know whom to sue.

"This is the underbelly of society," he said blankly, looking straight ahead as the Silverado teetered back into the northbound lane in front of us. On account of the reckless driving and the highway's deadly reputation, I was more than a bit on edge, protectively covering my privates at the slightest provocation from passing drivers.

The road was so deadly because it badly needed another two lanes of highway to make space for the incredible width of some of the semis hauling equipment up to Fort McMurray and also because there was simply too much traffic.

The promise of high-wage jobs in an otherwise slumbering economy attracted Canadians to Fort McMurray from all provinces. Alan told me he was getting paid like "a doctor" for simple engineering work. There are always opportunities in boomtowns, he told me, but there are also more than a few drawbacks. Alan had been working in oil and mining camps all his adult life, and he told me about the alcoholism, the drug addictions, the gambling, the prostitution: the products of having too much money and no real life. He was a recovering alcoholic. He'd seen it everywhere but nowhere as bad as Fort McMurray. The prostitutes were charging, according to Alan, three hundred dollars for twenty minutes of service. "They're there," he said. "You got choices."

Fort McMurray has increased its population tenfold since the early 1970s because of what's in the ground. Amid the muskeg and spruce roots is a substance as thick as peanut butter called bitumen (*bə-tyü-mən*), a mixture of clay, sand, water, and oil. Though there are several ways to get the bitumen, it is often mined in enormous man-made pits. The pits are dug and the bitumen is carried out with gigantic backhoes, bulldozers, and dump trucks. The only thing the oil companies are interested in with the bitumen is the oil. But separating the oil from the bitumen is a costly process, requiring tons of fresh water and natural gas.

The bitumen is essentially boiled at nearby refineries, a process that separates the oil from the clay and sand. Because of the high consumption of gas, the pollution of water, and the razing of the forest, not to mention the sheer scope of the operation (in which two million barrels of oil are produced every day), the tar sands are highly controversial, and the creation of the Keystone XL, which would pump this oil more quickly to Texas, would mean that the developed area of the tar sands would continue to spread.

After a few hours in the car with Alan, I began to feel comfortable enough with him to let him in on my plan while trying not to come across as the "I hate everything you do" radical environmentalist I sort of was.

"The workers don't give a rat's ass about the environment," Alan said. "The place is full of rednecks. Anyone with half a brain knows the country has a significant environmental problem. We just don't know what to do. If you start talking to people out here about the environment, they'll punch you. They'll get violent. They're here to make money. The people here are the worst sort."

Alan dropped me off at the Oil Sands Discovery Centre on the edge of town. It was late, and after hearing about the crime in town, I was scared of getting mugged in the middle of the night, so I chose to sleep where I figured no one would come wandering through: a thin stand of spruce and aspen poplars in between the Highway to Hell and a fenced-in industrial facility. There wasn't much of a chance of rain, so I didn't bother to set up my tent, sleeping instead on a few folds of cardboard that I'd used as hitchhiking signs. There was nothing between me and the stars except a few humble tree branches.

Throughout the night, my sleeping bag became saturated with dewdrops, which, by the morning, had turned into a frozen sheen of frost crystals. The whole night I listened to jacked-up trucks and semis hauling freight in and out of Fort McMurray.

Booming, indeed.

In the morning, I hobbled up the road and borrowed a Wi-Fi signal from a McDonalds's playroom, where I found an electrical socket. I checked my e-mail and looked at the map of Fort McMurray. I made my way to the post office to pick up a box of nine days' worth of food I'd mailed to myself from Denver.

Fort McMurray, despite bursting at the seams with people and cars and construction, did have a sort of northern charm. It was built atop a gently ascending hill alongside the Athabasca River, and it probably could have been a nice place if it wasn't for all the bustle, traffic, and crime. Alan had told me I'd never really get a good view of the tar sands from ground level, so I called one of the local aviation companies and scheduled a two-hundred-dollar flight tour. I hitch-hiked the twenty miles to the airstrip, and the pilot, a few years younger than I was, took me up in his four-seater Cessna 172.

I didn't realize it, but because the tar sands are so inconceivably large, I'd get to see only 10 percent of the pit-mining sites and none of the other operations that use different methods to extract the oil, such as steam-assisted gravity drainage, which account for about 50 percent of the operations. In northern Canada, there are as many as 1.63 tril-lion barrels of bitumen across 54,000 square miles of land, larger than the country of England.

We began the flight over the forest, a green hide of bristled spruce dappled with clusters of golden-yellow birch leaves and sprawling pools of dark-blue bog. The forest covered the earth with a thick layer of biota. Despite small sections that had been logged, the forest still felt wild, mysterious, inviting. The forest's autumnal hue had not yet bronzed into the crispy prewinter foliage that would portend winter's grim plans. They were the sort of woods you'd like to have rubbing up against your village, the sweet cool air and sleek orange leaves smell-ing of Halloween, hayrides, and backyard football. We flew over the Athabasca River, a deep, clear canoeist's dream, as thick and curva-ceous as a dragon's tail.

But the autumnal wonderland came to an abrupt end as we approached and then passed over an enormous tailings pond—a lifeless gray sea of sludge, the liquid residue of the bitumen-to-oil refining process. The ponds, which are more accurately described as lakes, bore no sign of bird, wind ripple, or fish. They were still, silent, dead. And they were everywhere. After the refining process, the oil industry creates these giant man-made lakes to store all the toxic fluids. As of 2010, the tailings ponds covered about seventy square miles of northern Alberta, with some ponds as big as 7,500 acres, or half the size of Manhattan. Migrating ducks are known to rest on the ponds, and because the ponds have killed thousands of them, the oil industry has placed scarecrows (dubbed "bit-u-men") wearing orange hazmat suits in the middle of them.

Beyond the pond was one of the pits, a breathtaking mud crater that was of such breadth it almost stretched to the edge of the viewable earth.

At worst, the scene was a war zone, the ground zero of some horrific city-destroying bomb. At best, it was a futuristic moon colony where imported laborers operated giant machinery, worked slave hours, and remorselessly plundered a place to which they have no emotional connection. How could this be here—in *Canada*? This seemed like the work of some deranged Third World tyrant bent on industrializing his nation at any cost, not the willful desecration of a whole ecozone carried out by an enlightened world power.

It was a mishmash of utter chaos and sublime sophistication. The pits appeared to have been dug, and redug, hundreds of feet into the ground. You could see the strata of previous digs, which looked like giant downward steps. The mined area was mostly a whitish gray or a drab desert brown. In the deepest parts of the mine, where trucks were scooping out fresh loads of dirt, was the bitumen, a gleaming gray black, so rich and wet and vibrant in color it brought to mind, despite all of the environmental hazards linked to it, an astounding fertility, a delicious loam, a shovel-deep scoop of life-dense Iowa soil.

Here it was. The whole reason everyone was here. *The oil.*

Peering down at the shimmering blackness, I thought I could begin to feel its unusual draw. Each scoop was money, security, prosperity. It was the world's fuel, its boggy-black lifeblood, the lubricant keeping our grand fossil-fuel experiment and consumer-capitalist machine humming.

Although the oil is very much a lifeless substance, you get a sense that it was, in fact, once a heap of screaming tropical life that had, over the ages, been composted down to the molecule, a rich blackness of potency, each bead a galaxy of condensed energy, sundrops that have lain in shadow ready to burst into life again at the heat of a flame. I almost sympathized with the oilmen: Why not reawaken this pool of sleeping wildness to let it live out one last moment of lightning-struck, horse-powered combustion before dissipating into airy nothingness? Our gooey remains don't deserve any worse.

There were thousands of workers down there bulldozing, maintaining roads, working in the refineries, working on restoration. From above, the men driving vehicles looked like ants, each acting independently yet functioning as a mind-bogglingly coordinated unit. We flew over a vast refinery, the shadow of our plane just a speck on the sprawling facility, the facility just a speck of the tar sands. There were lime-colored holding tanks in the shape of giant tuna cans, billowing towers, gray tubular chimneys coughing out clouds of smoke, a claptrap of pipes—pipes everywhere! It looked as if some buildings were made of them.

We flew over more curiosities: vast flat fields of blackness—about fifteen of them, all next to one another, each the size of a soccer field. (These were fields of "coke," a pure carbon that's left over from the refining process.) There were yellow sulfur pyramids being built into the sky, and splashes of water everywhere—ponds, puddles, small lakes. These weren't the dark-blue pools of the forest, but a vile sewer green. From the plane, the area vaguely smelled like tar. From the factories, a vapor spouted out into the atmosphere—not in a confident vertical but a peg-legged horizontal that fell clumsily onto the ground and swept across the terrain like a Great Plains miniduster.

Beyond the tailings ponds, the pits, the industrial facilities, the eerie sulfur pyramids, the fields of coke, the steely work camps, the Orwellian "reclaimed" zones—where they'd placed a herd of confused wood bison—was the forest. But the forest didn't seem like a forest anymore. It was just another zone soon to be plundered, just a thin stretch of healthfulness that had already resigned itself to its industrialized fate.

We flew back into Fort McMurray. I got off the plane feeling shell-shocked, dazed, rattled. I had no psychological precedent to draw from to help me process and make sense of what I'd just seen. It struck me that I didn't feel much at all. *Where is my anger? My hatred? My sadness?* More disturbing than the tar sands was my thought: *Do I even care?*

The human mind struggles to sympathize with a devastated landscape, especially one that was never our home. A whole ecosystem removed from the earth is an unbelievable sight. It's an abstract concept, and appreciating it requires more than just our eyes and ears. On first sight, we feel shock and awe and amazement, but I'd wager that only a few of us are overcome with the moral indignation that we'd originally expected to feel. It's not until afterward, when we've had time to think it over, to reflect on industry's shortsightedness, to imagine the exodus of animals, and to consider the implications for our climate—all nebulous, abstract things—that we begin to feel what we'd expected to feel and appreciate the enormity of what is being lost.

I retrieved my pack from the aviation company's office and drew up a new cardboard sign, this time reading SOUTH.

O riginally, I'd planned to start my walk in Fort McMurray, the very source of the oil, but after realizing that the existing underground Enbridge pipeline that links Fort McMurray to Hardisty would lead me through chin-high muskeg, a forbidden military zone, and forests teeming with black bears, I decided to change plans and use Hardisty, a small town on the Canadian prairie in central Alberta, as the beginning point of my hike. It would be, after all, the northern terminus of the Keystone XL. This way, the journey, I justified to myself, would be even more symbolically taut, as I was now focused entirely on the proposed route of the Keystone XL, which the soon-to-be-elected president was supposed to approve or reject after being sworn into office in a couple of months. Plus, this would now be a certifiable Great Plains Adventure, a walk from the northern extent of the continent's grasslands in central Alberta to its southern end down in Texas: a route that, as far as I knew, no one had ever walked.

I got a lift out of Fort McMurray with Eddie, a half-Native-American, half-Scandinavian oilman, who introduced himself to me as an alcoholic and a crack addict almost immediately after shaking hands. He said he'd been off crack for three months, a declaration that brought me about as much relief as the open can of Budweiser in his cup holder.

He was a giant of a man, a round-skulled grizzly bear whose meaty paws made his Dodge Ram's steering wheel look like a brittle halo. In dangerous situations, I, like most any guy—despite having no tested fighting skills whatsoever—imagine that I'm capable of unleashing a series of devastating martial-arts moves (that I'd unknowingly picked up and stored from movies) on a trio of adversaries. But Eddie was one of those guys who I knew could handily kick my ass—the sort who'd manhandle me into a headlock while letting out a breezy chuckle.

As usual with drivers, I was as polite and uncontroversial as I could be, sparing him the details of my visit and telling him that I was merely a writer (sort of true) who was gathering stories on the XL (sort of true, too).

He said he'd just quit his job in Fort McMurray despite the "disgusting" money he was making (four thousand dollars a week) so that he could see his kids, whom he'd seen for only eight weeks in the past year.

He said that after twelve hours of work the workers would come home to their camp dormitory, which was "more like a jail cell," to cope with the miseries of their way of life. "These guys, they're in a rut," Eddie said. "They can't get out of it. Some people smoke crack, and others, the crack smokes them. Fort McMurray takes your life, man. Fucking vicious cycle."

He dropped me off near the town of Lac La Biche. I walked the highway, jumped a barbed-wire fence, and set up my tent in a forest. I cleared away a few fallen logs on a relatively flat patch of ground before cooking up a meal of rice and beans sprinkled with Parmesan cheese. With a full belly, I squirmed into my tent, which was held in place by my two upright trekking poles.

When a leaf from the birch trees feathered down onto my tent, scraping against the fabric on its way to the forest floor, I'd wake up terrified, thinking someone was unzipping my door and trying to get in. When I realized it was just a leaf, my nerves were momentarily calmed, but that worry was merely replaced with another: *Winter is on my heels.*

I got off to an early start in the morning, mixing in my pot some water with dehydrated whole milk, throwing in a couple of palmfuls of granola cereal. I got on the highway, which was shrouded in heavy fog. The sun rose up in the east directly behind me. It was a scene of celestial perfection, the pale orange orb burning through the fog and hovering just feet above the double yellow line, illuminating the high-way to its most westward extent.

My second ride was with a pair of guys coming down from Fort McMurray headed to Edmonton, where they'd resume work with their landscaping business. The driver was adamantly pro-oil, telling me about all the jobs pipelines create and how men can support their families with the money. "There will be jobs," he said. "It's going to happen."

He said that anyone who uses oil shouldn't complain about oil.

"Hypocrites," he said, though he said I was an exception since I'd be walking the pipe.

Was I anti-oil? The tar sands and the Keystone XL struck me as pretty terrible ideas, but how could I be anti-oil when all of my gear, clothes, and food were made with, made of, or transported by oil? I was wearing nylon pants and a polyester shirt, which were materials made from oil. Oil was in my pack, my shoes, my trekking poles. I'd originally wanted to travel the XL without using any oil. But where would I, for instance, get shoes that weren't shipped with oil? How could I get food without any trace of oil? I could bring a rifle and hunt rabbits and deer, but what oil-run machine had cut the wood for the stock? What fuel ran the furnace that shaped the barrel? Where did the lead come from? Oil was everywhere; it was in everything. And going without oil or coal or natural gas was, on this hike and in life in general, pretty much impossible.

The more I thought about it, the more I thought his assertion that "no one who uses oil can complain about it" was just a handy little line to silence heresy. Indeed, let's acknowledge that oil is a big part of our lives, but let's not forget that oil and oil's fossil-fuel cousins are creating some rather massive problems. Seen in this light, some nuanced criticism of the fuel seems warranted.

But he was kind enough to give me a ride, so I swallowed my objections and listened politely.

Later, I'd get rides with a potato farmer, a teacher, a carpenter, and a truck driver. I'd broach the subject of the XL, always in respectful, nonpartisan, I'd-best-not-get-my-ass-kicked ways, and their opinions seemed to land somewhere in between indifference and wholehearted support of the pipeline.

During all of my rides, the conversation revolved around work. Work on oil rigs for fourteen hours straight. Hammering nails in forty-below in steel-toed boots. Snowplowing. Construction. Mining. Potato picking. Work, work, work. That's what everyone talked about. There was a sort of placid resignation that work consumed almost the entirety of their lives, and there was something admirably wholesome about their unthinking diligence. But there was something sad about it, too. Where was the enlightened heresy, the impassioned religion, the wildness that makes you think, *Wow, now there's a person?* It was just work. A lot of work. Hard work. A pipeline, to them, wasn't something to debate. It was just someone else's work.

5.

The Gunmen

September 24, 2012

←→

H ardisty didn't seem at all like one of North America's major pipe-line hubs, but in addition to being the potential fountainhead of the Keystone XL, Hardisty, population 639, was, in fact, the cross-roads of a number of other pipelines that ran beneath the ground. On its outskirts was an oil depot of white holding tanks, known as a "tank farm."

Hardisty may have a hard industrial exterior, but there is also a soft inner core of simple homes and an endearing Main Street lined down the middle with pots overflowing with purple flowers. The li-brary was closed, so I sat behind it, pilfering Internet access to put up a blog entry and charging up my camera with an outdoor electrical socket. Meanwhile, I took everything out of my pack to let the con-tents dry from the morning dew, repacking everything carefully, plac-ing items so that the weight was distributed equally on both sides. I put a few handy items toward the top, including my rain suit and a day's worth of snacks, so that they could be retrieved with ease. I walked to the town's convenience store so I could use the bathroom.

"No pack!" yelled the Asian storeowner. "You leave pack outside."

I didn't want to begin my trip flustered and frantic for a bathroom, though I had no choice but to leave the store, extend my trekking poles (which made me feel awfully self-conscious), and head off down the road in search of an increasingly rare cluster of trees.

I was again mystified by how I was going to pull this off. The farther south I went, the fewer trees I saw, and finding hidden camping spots was getting harder and harder. It reminded me of that hauntingly dry and desolate hay-and-cow landscape I'd seen in Montana. The landscape was now almost entirely prairie: cow pasture, hay fields, grasslands. There were just a few pockets of woods here and there, mostly around creeks and lakes.

Where will I sleep? Where will I get my water? Will landowners shoot me for trespassing on their property? *One step at a time, man!* I thought. *One step at a time . . .*

I suppose now's as good a time as any to draw a self-portrait of the author. He stands five feet eight-and-a-half inches tall (rounded up to five nine, he tells himself, for purposes of "simplification") and weighs in at one eighty, cutting a mostly normal, if forgettable, figure. He has a few uncombed locks of brown hair and green eyes, one of which has a scar above it. (As a teen, in baseball practice, I was so mesmerized with the twirling laces of a fly ball that I forgot to try to catch it with my glove.)

When in society, the author makes a point to attend to all the standards of hygiene and appearance, but when left to himself, he gladly foregoes the rituals of bathing and changing his underwear, as well as shaving his beard, which, when left unperturbed, bears wisps of every imaginable hair color in homage to his blended European ancestry.

Athletically, his modest frame prohibits him from ever dreaming of dunking a basketball or maneuvering past an NFL lineman, but he was endowed with a sturdy, well-proportioned averageness: good for carrying weight, tolerating cold, and enduring hours of drudgery. (He hails from a family of Scots coal miners and probably would have functioned well as one if he'd been born in a less fortunate age.)

The author lacks talents in all arts, is master of no skills, jack of no trades, but claims an expertise in loafing, staring into space, binge-watching Netflix TV shows, and taking catnaps. He walks with a straightened back in public, slouches in private, and when he's up reading at night, he has the bad habit of pinching out bouquets of nose hairs for no clear reason. While most anyone who's met him would consider him a "nice young man," he knows that's not always true (as he's predisposed to quietly wallowing in misanthropy and judging others—personal traits, the author wants to assure the reader, *he's working on*).

Except for his being unaffiliated with any Christian church, he thought his being a white, straight, American male would prove to be an advantageous demographical makeup for a trek through the Great Plains states—a region that does not have a reputation for ethnic and cultural diversity—as horrible as all that sounds.

. . .

The Keystone XL had yet to be placed in the ground, so there was no clear path for me to follow. I'd have to rely almost entirely on my compass needle and topographic maps for navigation. For much of the Canadian leg of my journey, though, the XL would parallel preexisting pipelines. Having once lived next to the Alaska pipeline, which stretches eight hundred miles from Alaska's northern coast to its southern, I figured this would mean I'd have a big aboveground pipe to follow and a crunchy gravel road next to it on which I'd walk. But here in Alberta, even though there are many pipelines, it's almost impossible to tell where these pipes are since they had all been buried underground. (I didn't know this at the time, but there are 150,000 miles of oil pipelines in the United States alone. Add gas pipelines, and we have more than 1.7 million miles of pipes. These are our veiled veins, silently moving fossil fuels beneath the ground like blood beneath skin.)

It was an exceptionally hot and sunny fall day, so I generously applied sunscreen and lip balm as I ambled along Highway 13. The back of my shirt became soaked in sweat, and I ran out of water within a couple of hours. What few water sources I found didn't appear to be remotely potable, so I determined to ask for water at the next house. But out here on the barren prairie, there were miles between homes. At the first one I came across, horses trotted over and slung their heads over a wooden horizontal fence beam. When I went to touch their soft nostrils, they pulled their heads back coyly. A sheepdog with hackles and a low growl peered at me fearfully as I approached the house. I called out, "Hello!" A middle-aged woman in a flannel shirt came out and pulled up on the well lever, pouring the first gush of tepid water into a couple of buckets so that I could get the "cool stuff."

Her father came out, and he asked me where I was going. I said I was walking to Texas and that today was my first day.

"How about that," he said.

I'd been confounded with the absence of trees, so at the next house I asked the homeowner, "Are there any more woods south of here?"

He snickered to himself and, despite my apparent concern, reported with relish, "From here on down, there ain't nothin' but cold-ass prairie."

On the road, the muscles in my right buttock felt as if they'd tied themselves into a hideous knot. I carried a heaviness there, a lump of coal that was mostly tolerable except for a hot spasm every few minutes. My hip belt on my backpack rubbed my hips a raw pink so, in consideration of all of my first-day ailments, I decided to call it a night when I saw a scattering of maples up ahead, just short of the town of Amisk. Thirteen miles on my first day, I calculated. Not bad.

The next day, I kept on walking in the same southeasterly direction, except now I was on a railroad track, taking shorter steps so my feet could comfortably fall on the wooden planks rather than the loose gravel. I walked along the edge of Shorncliffe Lake, still on the tracks, and a few cows spotted me from behind a barbed-wire fence and took off in a panic, triggering a hundred-strong pell-mell stampede into the woods. A train thundered from behind me, so I scampered into the woods, where I watched it roll past.

I camped in woods south of a town called Czar. After Czar, the highway turned straight south, so to continue my southeasterly direction I'd have to finally get off the road system and venture out into open country. I'd have to trespass.

I walked south on the highway for a bit, looking for just the right place to climb over the barbed-wire fence (which was about four feet high). When no houses were visible and when no trucks were passing, doing my best not to get caught, I hopped the fence and walked a good distance from the road as quickly as I could.

I was walking over a wide, hilly grassland. The grass was still moist from the morning dew, so my shoes and socks quickly became saturated, as did my pants up to my knees. But I didn't mind. Now that I was off the hard asphalt and onto soft ground, there was a knee-happy bounce to my step.

Suddenly, I figured that I was going to be okay. Why had I worried myself sick about trespassing? *The plains are so wide open, so big, so barren. I'm not going to get shot out here. This is grassland, not swampland. These are cows, not bison. This is twenty-first-century North America. The wild animals—the cougars, the grizzlies, the wolves—have been gone for more than a century.*

I walked up and down rolling country. The mounds of earth weren't big enough to be called hills, but they formed a smooth, never-flat, gently sloping terrain. So long as I didn't conspicuously stand on top of any of these hills, I knew I could travel in between the hill crests, where I'd probably go unnoticed. Ahead was a cluster of spruce and hardwoods, and as I got closer, I saw the dark-brown rump of a horse. The presence of a horse in this rolling grass country didn't seem all that unusual, so I kept up my pace and intended to pass it by, imagining myself courteously nodding to it in midstride.

It heard my approaching footsteps and broke through the woods, the leaves shuddering as the trees rocked violently to each side. It lumbered out into the open and eyed me from its side. It had antlers that looked like an upside-down set of chandeliers and a low hanging dewlap, a kingly double chin. The horse, which turned out to be a bull moose, was standing perfectly still.

Having lived up in Alaska, I knew that spotting a moose was no reason to get alarmed. I kept my distance, snapped a quick photo, and took a detour to the right alongside another set of woods. Then there was another explosion in the woods: splitting bark, trampled logs, the forest rattling with alarm. I'd unknowingly spooked a cow moose—a female moose—which thrashed through the woods. The sight of the fleeing animal had upset the bull moose, which was now running toward me, its gargantuan gray-brown body lurching over the grass.

It was holding its head high, armored with a pointy rack, and coming at me not quite at a sprint but at a cocky, testosterone-fueled trot, which was just as scary.

There's probably only one reasonable thing you could do when you're unarmed and a thousand-pound mammal is charging at you— especially when that animal has the option of either trampling you with its bone-shattering hooves or knocking you senseless with its helmet of baseball bats. And that one reasonable thing is to run for your life as fast you can in a completely unironic, unabashed, uncaring-if-footage-of-this-is-going-to-end-up-on-YouTube sort of way.

So I ran. I ran as fast as I could, which, honestly, wasn't all that fast with my forty-pound pack. So I shuffled forward toward another set of trees, where I hoped some long-lost "my ancestors were monkeys" tree-climbing instincts would instantaneously kick in. My buttock spasmed, sending an arrowhead of pain through my hindquarter. I raced on but now felt as if some invisible tether were yanking me to the ground at the worst possible second.

Before long, the moose relented. I stood on top of a grassy hill and watched it canter back into the woods, holding up its head with an undisguised impertinence, clearly satisfied with how events had played out even if his goriest longings had gone unquenched.

Anyone who has scared away, outwitted, or outrun a wild animal bigger than they are surely has had the urge to belt out a barbarian roar in the victorious wake of all that suspense. I held in my roar to preserve my stealth, but I was no less exhilarated. Yet I still couldn't help but again question the feasibility of my hike. I'd only been trespassing for an hour and I had already been charged by a prehistoric beast. An hour! I still had like four months to go!

I was now in cow and bull country. There were gangs of cows everywhere. They were the sort of cows with black or brown bodies whose perfectly white faces were worn like demonic masks. Some were in large groups of twenty or more, each with their heads lowered munching on grass and looking as if they had a thick fifth limb. There were other cows all by themselves, and mothers with calves by their sides.

I deliberately walked alongside a fence so that I'd be able to jump to the other side if I was attacked. From about a hundred yards behind me, a horde of about twenty cows was slowly making its way toward me. I picked up my pace, eventually outwalking them. I tossed my pack over a fence and climbed the wire with my feet, bracing my arm against the wooden fence post before finally leaping over the fence down onto the ground and strapping the pack onto my back again.

Soon, a group of about six cows with two calves was paralleling me. I was out in the open now.

When I stopped, they stopped. When I walked, they walked. What did they have in mind? What are they doing?

"Go away, cows!" I yelled. "Go away!"

That didn't work so I changed my tone. "You're a bunch of sweethearts. You're going to leave me alone now, okay?"

They continued to parallel me until their attention was drawn to an especially lush patch of grass.

I walked through woods, occasionally hearing thuds of frightened hooves or seeing the movement of some black shadow behind layers of trees. I studied every noise nervously. I felt as if I could be blindsided any second. These weren't just cows, but cunning velociraptors hunting me from my blind spots.

I broke through the stand of woods, and ahead of me was a small lake, so I had to make a decision about which way to go around it. I went to the left, but a gang of bulls, feeling comfort in numbers, began to amble my way. I changed direction and, without any option, walked toward another group of cows standing still and watching me with an unflinching and disturbing curiosity. I walked directly toward them. These cows continued to stare until finally, as if stung by wasps, they clumsily swung their heads around and took off in the opposite direction at a respectable gallop.

I was sweating profusely again, and I'd drunk all of my water so, without any better idea, I dropped my pack by the lake and pulled out my three collapsible one-liter water bottles. The edge of the lake was muddy and gouged by cow hooves. I quickly dipped my bottles into the lake and poured my chlorine dioxide mix in to purify the water. Twenty cows from the opposite wooded shore unleashed deep guttural moans. The deepness of a cow's moan seems only partly audible: We're blasted by the rich full-throated bass, some of which is processed by our ears, but the rest can only be felt reverberating through our bowels.

The more I walked, the wilder the terrain got. There were fewer fences, no roads, no trails, not even a footstep or tire track. I walked alongside another lake, and to the right of me a light-gray wolf—or a giant coyote, I wasn't sure which—broke out from the bush, ran in front of me, and stormed across the prairie at a speed that didn't slow for as long as I watched it.

My heart couldn't take it anymore. It was as if it had been stabbed by surprise over and over in just a matter of hours. I looked into the thick of the woods, and without realizing what I was doing, I pulled out my jackknife and, while gripping it firmly in one hand, screamed—as if to the whole animal kingdom—"C'MON! C'MON!" My fear had been transfigured into a blood-curdling, full-throated berserker rage. "Bring it on!" I yelled lustily, prepared to pierce the next charging ungulate or canine with four inches of cool, razor-sharp steel.

I continued on, the tops of my feet beginning to feel uncomfortably hot and prickly. I still had two hours of daylight so I pushed on. All the other parts of my body—my back, hips, and shoulders—were in good shape. I was now out in the open, walking up and over gentle mounds covered in the shaggy wildness of countless species of grass, weed, and flower, none of which I could name. I felt safer out in the open where I could see all around me, so I was determined to stay away from the woods.

What hills! The Alberta prairie was not the oppressively flat landscape I'd envisioned. The prairie, I could see, could be hilly, contoured with gently undulating mounds of grassy earth, as unimposing as the chocolatey soil turned by a farmer's plow. Thick but narrow forests adjoined neighboring hills, and scattered everywhere were ponds, each receding with the ongoing drought, revealing a rime of salt along the edges.

I climbed the tallest hill, swirled in a slow 360, and didn't see one house or farm or road. The land everywhere was the color of butterscotch.

I could have moved into one of the still-existing plains towns along the route of the XL, or I could have driven the roads of the prairie, but I wanted to slow myself to a steady march and go only where my legs could take me. A sort of "traveling idler," the walker is able—unlike the cyclist, motorist, and aviator—to stop and examine, mull and ponder, photograph and reflect, all at the slightest provocation. And—barring unfordable rivers and unscalable mountains—he can go wherever he damn well pleases.

Between the autumn colors and the sepia twilight cast onto the hills by rays of the setting sun, I could momentarily forget my day's many scares and feel a tired thankfulness—a reminder that despite whatever trials lay ahead I got to be struck dumb every day by sights that felt like they'd been made for me, each color, each texture, each arrangement of tree and grass and pond a composition that was mine during that moment, and for those few that would etch themselves into the tablet of my memory, mine forever. *I get to walk over this every day?* I thought.

I wanted to keep walking, but my toes got sorer as the evening wore on. I set up my tent behind a cluster of trees that was tightly packed with bushes and immature hardwoods, leaving little room for a tent. I figured sleeping out in the open wouldn't be a big deal in a land so empty of people.

I spread out my tent on the ground, driving stakes in with a rock at the head and foot of the tent. Then I stuck one of my trekking poles beneath the tent roof, stretched out one side of the tent, and hammered another stake into the ground. I did the same on the opposite end, and I finally had my small, ultralight, and so-far-trusty one-person tent all set up.

I got in and immediately took off my socks and shoes to examine what was happening to my feet. The tops of my feet and toes were a bright pink, as if the topmost layer of skin had been rubbed away. They were covered in dirt and specks of green wool from my socks. I pulled out my med kit, found a few packets of rubbing-alcohol towelettes, and rubbed my wounds clean in a vaguely enjoyable, wrinkly faced pain. I kept my feet propped up on my backpack to let them air out while I turned on my iPad to resume reading *The Lord of the Rings*, which I'd started a few nights before.

I heard a distant rumbling behind me and it was getting louder and louder. *That isn't what I think it is, is it?* It was a truck. My tent, on this side of the woods, was in full view. Here I am, in practically the middle of nowhere, and I've picked a camping spot right next to one of the very few gravel roads in the area! I hadn't seen the road because I was camped in a depressed hollow, and the road was clearly up atop a nearby ridge line just twenty yards away that I hadn't inspected.

I heard the car doors open, slam shut, and then the swishy crunch of feet on gravel.

I quietly reached over and gripped my jackknife and bear spray.

"Whew-hoo! I'm gonna shoot up everything that moves!" proclaimed a young man. "Where's my shotgun?"

"Got your twelve-gauge, Randy?" asked another.

I listened to a group of young men, probably in their late teens or early twenties, discussing the respective merits of their guns with an ardor I thought inappropriate for anything other than a lover. The conversation struck me as preposterously stereotypical—the sort of mindless gun-loving jabber that city folk imagine country hicks engage in.

I thought about calling out hello and introducing myself, but when I heard a barrage of gunfire overhead, I knew I had no option but to lie still with my eyes tightly sealed.

Gunshots, loud booming gunshots, whistled overhead.

BANG! BANG! BANG!

What could I do at that point? Could I bellow hello above the din of exploding shells? Or should I remain quiet? If I yelled, I worried that after their successful discharge of arms, in the very midst of their orgasm of masculinity, they might very well thoughtlessly mow me down as if I were nothing more than a jumble of video-game pixels. I chose to remain still.

They fired a few more shots and, much to my relief, got back into the truck and sped away. I scurried out of the tent and tore it down for fear that they'd spot it on their drive back. I crawled along the ground into the brush, dragging the tent and all its contents behind me as if it were an animal carcass. My feet, which I'd just carefully cleaned, were once again covered in dirt. I lay flat on my back, taking cover among a few low bushes.

Until I was sure they were gone for good, I promised myself I wouldn't budge an inch. I waited ten minutes, then thirty, then an hour. In the distance I could hear the *putt-putt* of their rifles and shotguns. And closer by, I could hear the gentle rustle of the few mice and birds that lived in this tiny glade, and felt a rare sense of kinship as I, too, was hunkered down, hiding, and scared for my life.

Eventually, the young men came back and got out of their truck at the same spot. I couldn't see them, and I knew not to show the slightest movement. Fear of getting shot was more than outweighing my desire to catch a glimpse of them.

There wasn't much talk this time except from someone who was likely a mentally challenged member of the party, who called out, "Let's go home! I'm hungry for some supper!" It was then that I realized that they were probably sweet people, taking their slower brother out to shoot with them.

When they took off down the road again, it was sufficiently dark, so I set up my tent again, this time in the bushes. I lay awake, struggling to fall asleep, thinking of moose and cows and coyotes and shooting galleries and cold-ass prairie. The Great Plains.

What is this place?

6.

The Great Plains

←→

What are we to do with the term "Great Plains"? The problem begins with its puzzling plurality. Just how many plains are there? Two? Twenty? Two thousand? If it's all more or less flat or flattish—as the term implies—shouldn't they just be called the "Great Plain"? For good reason we don't call the Sahara the Sahara Desert*s* or the Amazon the Amazon River*s*.

The next problem is with our noun "plain." While "plain" does, in fact, accurately describe a "large area of flatland with few trees," the word, through association with its other and less flattering definitions, leaves us with the feeling that the plains are (in addition to being treeless) unexceptional, unexciting, unremarkable. *Plain.* It would be just as well to refer to the area as the "Great Boring." If you feel I'm being hyperbolic or that I'm trifling about semantics, call your lover a "flowery meadow" in one sentence and the "Great Plain" in the next, and see if she responds differently.

The final problem lies with the Plains' grandiloquent qualifier, "Great," which, sadly, does nothing to conjure an image of *greatness* but merely emphasizes the area's great *vastness*. Not only are the Plains plain, but they're *enormously* plain. And how could we fault anyone for making such an assessment after driving almost ten hours from Kansas City to Denver over the flat, windy, and nearly bendless I-70?

There's no question that the Great Plains are enormous. They stretch 2,500 miles from north to south and 600 miles east to west. They encompass huge sections of the Canadian provinces of Alberta, Saskatchewan, and Manitoba, and pretty much the whole states of North Dakota, South Dakota, Nebraska, Kansas, Oklahoma, and Texas. They also include sections of Montana, Wyoming, Colorado, and New Mexico to the west, and Minnesota, Iowa, and Missouri to the east. The plains cover about a fifth of Canada and the United States, making it the second largest ecosystem on the continent after the boreal forest.

The plains aren't to be mistaken with the "Midwest," an awkward and rather arbitrary term that includes tree-and-leaf states as far east as Ohio and, just to confuse matters, does, in fact, include a few Great Plains states. For our purposes, all we need to know is that the Great Plains describe America's Great Prairie (a better term, in my view), which, until relatively recently, was a vast, almost-unbroken grassland, a thirty-million-strong buffalo paradise.

Despite its immense size, the Great Plains remain to this day mostly uninhabited, containing just 3 percent of the U.S. population, with many counties containing less than one person per square mile.

When you're driving across Kansas, it's reasonable to conclude that the Plains are and always have been a place of great emptiness, boredom, and plainness.

For 55 million years (545 million to 490 million years ago), the plains were actually a great sea. This sea would come and go with changing climates and tectonic shifts, leaving behind gentle hills of sand, silt, and shells, which are now the wavy contours of our great grasslands.

During this period of dramatic tectonic plate movement, the plains to the west were thrust skyward, forming the Rocky Mountains. The Rockies began to erode as soon as they emerged, crumbling, blowing away, and being carried down the mountainside by creeks and rivers. The Great Plains were the giant dustbin that collected all the erosion from the newly formed and hardly tidy Rockies, which filled in the plains sea with piles of mud, sand, and volcanic ash.

About 225 million years ago, the area teemed with dinosaurs and verdant woodlands. The long-necked *Brachiosaurus*, weighing in at upwards of 176,000 pounds, yanked leaves from tall treetops, and the thick-bodied *Stegosaurus*, with its armored spine, snacked on vegetation closer to ground. After the plains were drowned by yet another ocean, gushing around the Rockies during the Cretaceous (between 145 million and 65 million years ago), the ocean receded again, opening up a wide and rolling soon-to-be-jungle expanse for herds of *Triceratops* and the solitary *Tyrannosaurus rex* that hunted them. Moths and bees inhabited the air while the *Quetzalcoatlus*, with its more than thirty-foot wingspan, soared in the skies. Frogs and salamanders were around then, too, as were a few of our justifiably terrified mouse-size mammalian ancestors.

When the dinosaurs went extinct, these underground mammals emerged and finally had their opportunity to evolve and take hold of the plains. About 45 million years ago, the plains—warm, subtropical, and covered by lush forest—were populated with leaping monkeys, jittery squirrels, chubby *Brontotheriidae* (a rhinolike beast with knobby horns and sharp tusks), and the *Orohippus* (a horse the size of a sheep-dog that had four toes on its front feet and three on its back). As with all epochs, this one would come to an end. But this time it wasn't be-cause of a drowning ocean or a devastating meteor strike. This time it got cold.

The continent that once combined Antarctica and Australia broke apart, creating a change in ocean currents that caused the global tem-perature to drop eighteen degrees Fahrenheit over the course of the next million years. The plains were now cooler and drier: bad for jun-gles but ideal for grasses. Hanging out around the rare river—a critical source of water on the increasingly arid plains—were yet more daz-zlingly interesting mammals: miniature rhinos the size of pigs; several species of horses the size of dogs; camels; ancient beavers that made homes by burrowing corkscrew tunnels into the prairie—all hunted by dogs and saber-toothed cats.

The plains continued to dry, causing what trees there were to wither and all but destroying everyone's hiding places. On the plains, it wasn't just the strong that survived. It was the quick. The animals, without the dense cover of a forest, became especially fleet of foot, like the still-existing pronghorn—a North American original and the fastest animal in the hemisphere, which runs with its mouth open, sucking oxygen down a wide windpipe into giant lungs, allowing it to run at speeds of up to sixty miles per hour to evade its now-extinct adversary—the North American cheetah.

The earth cooled and the top third of North America was gradu-ally smothered in snow, which compacted into ice, which turned into enormous glaciers two miles high. ("[T]hat's about the height, from base to peak, of Mount Everest," writes natural historian Candace Savage.)* As far south as Kansas, glaciers advanced and retreated numerous times with changing global temperatures. The wind blasted the plains where the glaciers had been, drumming up horrific dust storms of bare silt and sand, and dumping them in giant mounds that would form what are today the sandhills of Nebraska and Alberta.

The ice began its final departure 18,000 years ago, a retreat that lasted some 10,000 years, leaving tundra to the north and a coniferous forest to the south that was inhabited by white-tailed and mule deer, pronghorns, caribou, black bears, lions, cheetahs, saber-toothed cats, dire wolves, ground sloths, horses, camels, llamas, giant beavers (the size of black bears), woolly mammoths, and mastodons.

The Ice Age elephants were migrants from Eurasia, tramping over the Bering land bridge from modern-day Russia into Alaska. When the climate warmed, a narrow passageway had opened up through the ice that led straight from Alaska to the plains. Along with the elephants came elk, grizzlies, moose, and bison. The Eurasian bison, with their long curvy horns (drawn in caves in southern France), would evolve in North America, becoming the more compact, shorter-horned species we know today, *Bison bison*. About 13,000 years ago, western North America had a richer species diversity than Africa does today.

It's unclear exactly when the first humans arrived in North America, but we know that we were established on the plains 11,000 years ago, having migrated with the animals over the Bering land bridge.

The plains were undergoing yet another massive change: As hu-

---

* Special credit is due to Candace Savage for her admirable work on the natural history of the Great Plains in *Prairie: A Natural History*.

mans were arriving, the climate was warming and the glaciers were receding. The Rockies captured moisture that blew over from the Pacific, greedily keeping the rains to themselves and, in so doing, parching the poor plains, which now receive only sixteen to twenty-four inches of precipitation a year, which is just enough to keep them from becoming a desert but not enough to support a full-fledged forest. Many of the giant mammals (perhaps because of changes in climate and the presence of humans) went extinct.

Some of the first human arrivals, the Clovis people, brought with them advanced spear-making technologies perfect for hunting big-game animals such as the woolly mammoth. But their culture eventually went extinct along with the animals they depended on.

The natives adapted to new conditions: They hunted, gathered, and lived nomadic lifestyles, moving when the climate or the travels of animals compelled them to. By AD 1000, natives were farming on the plains, growing corn, beans, squash, and sunflowers, and living in houses made of wood and earthen materials.

By the time the Spanish arrived in the 1500s, close to one hundred generations of people had lived and died on the plains. In the five centuries before European contact, between 50 and 200 million natives had lived in North America.

The Spanish, as gold hungry and gullible as ever, heard rumors of the Seven Cities of Cibola, where doorways were supposedly studded with turquoise and the land laden with gold. In 1540, Francisco Vázquez de Coronado embarked on an expedition from Compostela, Mexico, to find Cibola, which, it turned out, had neither seven cities nor gold. The Spanish did, however, find an Indian whom they dubbed the Turk for his likeness to a Turkish man. The Turk told them of another golden city called Quivira—this one on the plains. So began the first plains journey led by a European.

The Spaniards took their horses over the only roads known to the plains—the sprawling paths of the buffalo, an animal that the Spanish unimaginatively referred to as a "cow." But Quivira didn't have any gold either, only some healthy-looking and near-naked Wichita Indians who were living close to modern-day Great Bend, Kansas. We can only guess how Coronado felt after his long and pointless march. The poor Turk surely must have recognized by then the predicament he was in, dealing with a disappointed Spanish explorer—all of whom, we can infer from history, seemed to have listed "prone to genocidal rampage" and "psychopathy" on their résumés. Under prosecution (which may or may not have included an iron garrote around the Turk's neck), the Turk confessed that he'd misled the expedition, which very well could have been true, considering that the Turk's only hope would have been to guide the expedition over the desolate plains with the hope that the plains would kill the witless Spaniards before they killed him. In the end, the expedition didn't end well for anyone. Coronado, embarrassed, sent a disappointed letter to his king, and the Turk was, according to the Spaniards' point of view, appropriately strangled.

Thereafter, the Spanish, having learned their lesson, more or less left the plains alone. But their influence would change the natives' way of life for centuries. Their horses, lost or abandoned during these early expeditions, were unintentionally reintroduced to the plains after an absence of about 11,000 years. The horse took to the plains as if it had never been gone. Over the next few centuries, wild horse populations boomed, and the natives taught themselves to become, arguably, the most skilled horsemen on the planet. Captain Randolph Marcy, in his nineteenth-century memoir, describes his amazement upon witnessing a native "throwing himself entirely upon one side of his horse and discharging his arrows with great rapidity toward the opposite side from beneath the animal's neck while he is at full speed." Previously, the plains peoples lived a partly sedentary life in farming villages. When the tribes had to move around, dogs would haul their possessions with a travois (a sled made of two long poles that dragged along the ground). But with the horse, they became a truly mobile people and even better buffalo hunters.

The tribes of the plains—the Blackfoot, Comanche, Lakota, Crow, Apache, Kiowa, and many more—flourished. Populations boomed, and between the horse and the introduction of the rifle, the Indians grew more warlike in their efforts to secure territory. After battles, warriors notched sticks to record their most daring feats.

For westward American pioneers, the plains were a hazardous no-man's-land, a frontier that was ultimately out of reach unless you were lucky enough to take part in one of a few government-funded expeditions like Lewis and Clark's 1804 Corps of Discovery journey.

Maps referred to the plains as the "Great American Desert" from 1820 through 1858, and the only visitors to the plains were those who were passing through en route to someplace else. The plains, to them, were merely an obstacle on their quests to find gold or religious freedom in the west. By 1843, the Oregon Trail was well established, but travelers faced many hardships: disease, Indian attacks, hypothermia, and drowning. The problem of transportation over the dry plains was so severe that U.S. Secretary of War Jefferson Davis began overseeing the introduction of seventy-five camels in 1855, which were to serve the army's transportation needs.

The Homestead Act was passed in 1862, giving homesteaders free plains land if they could survive on it for five years. After the Civil War, homesteaders from east of the Mississippi moved west in droves. The U.S. military, now with spare time on its hands, proceeded to break treaties and slaughter the natives, most notably in 1890 at Wounded Knee in South Dakota, where several hundred men, women, and children were gunned down. In just a matter of years, the natives were pushed onto reservations, railways were built, the buffalo were almost driven to extinction, and white people—who knew nothing about the plains, its climate, its grasses, or its wildlife—moved in to raise cattle and farm.

By the 1870s, the plains had become cattle country. The ranchers enjoyed a few brief years of a wide-open landscape, but in 1874, the first piece of barbed wire was strung up, and in the decades that followed, the landscape would be divided by visible lines of private property.

Wheat farming supplanted ranching as the dominant industry of the plains in places, and between 1880 and 1925, two hundred million acres of plains land was homesteaded, half of which was considered marginal farmland.

Poor farming techniques mixed with years of drought created the "black blizzards"—the dust storms of the 1930s. By the end of the decade, the most ferocious of the black blizzards ceased tormenting the plains, but the twentieth century and beyond has not been kind to the land or its people. Because of the vagaries of plains farming, many farmers were forced off their land to make way for high-tech industrial agriculture. With bigger and better equipment, not to mention the development of herbicides and pesticides, farmers could farm larger expanses of land with fewer workers. Since the plains' high-population heyday of the 1920s, farming populations have fallen 80 percent. Despite the exodus of farmers, by 2007 the plains made up 37 percent of U.S. farmland, producing 21 percent of our corn, 52 percent of our wheat, 93 percent of our canola, and 50 percent of our cattle. The plains are unquestionably our breadbasket even if the basket is oozing over with goopy corn syrup.

Because of the private-property and farming bonanza, fifty-five grassland species are endangered or threatened, 465,000 square miles of natural grasslands have been destroyed (an area bigger than Texas and California put together), and because of that, 60 percent of bird species that rely on the plains are in decline. The grizzly and wolf have disappeared, and the prairie dogs live on only 1 percent of the range they had a century ago. Their predators, the black-footed ferret and swift fox, approach extinction. Except for a few protected herds here and there, the bison no longer roam free, and since most of the plains are strung up with barbed wire, not much of anything, save for leaping ungulates such as deer and pronghorn, roams free anymore.

At the time of my walk, I didn't know much of the land's history. All of it dwelled beneath the ground, and atop it I could see only pale-green grasses serenely tossing back and forth with the wind. But I knew I wasn't walking across just rangeland or developed lands, but across a sort of half-tamed wilderness, where cows dwell and fences hold in herds, but where coyotes and the occasional moose roam; where there is no cover from the whirlwinds of summer twisters or the cold sting of unforgiving winters; where you could get killed for doing something *stupid*.

I wasn't walking across private property; I was walking through an undesignated national park. I was walking across the Heartland—a region most Americans don't think about but that's a part of us all: It feeds us, irrigates us, powers our cars and planes, and bears some of the best and worst of our history as a people. It's a metaphor that is unsettlingly real: What happens to our country's core will affect the rest of the body. What was once a great no-man's-land to Americans—the Great American Desert—is no longer a westward frontier but rather the wide chest that contains our beating, sometimes stuttering heart.

7.

The Teacher

CONSORT, ALBERTA—1,858 MILES TO GO

September 27, 2012

←→

Just after dawn, I was lying in a ditch positioning moleskin on my blistered toes and the tops of my burning feet. A storm of black-birds descended on the field next to me, roosting and gregariously cawing on a golden bale of hay.

My feet were burning with a prickly pain that grew more unbear-able by the minute. When I ran out of moleskin, I wrapped my toes with the tiny roll of duct tape I'd brought, which did nothing for the pain, but made them look like metallic Tin Man toes.

I staggered into the town of Consort (pop. 689), where I wandered into a farm-and-ranch-supply store. Six older men were sitting in a circle of folding chairs drinking coffee. I asked where I could find a pharmacy, and they directed me to the center of town. The pharmacist explained that my problem wasn't chafing exactly, which I'd assumed, but a fungus. He recommended two creams for thirty dollars.

Since I was in town, I figured that I'd check my e-mail at the local library, which was located in the town's high school. A teacher named Harold, young and dapper with blond hair, excitedly asked what I was doing with my big pack and trekking poles, and if I'd like to have dinner with his family that evening, which I enthusiastically agreed to.

Meanwhile, I sat on a toilet in the boys' restroom, carefully applying the creams. My feet were a mess. I ran my fingers over crusted red scars rubbed raw across my toe knuckles and the tops of my feet. Underneath most of my toes were blisters. I might as well have been walking on coals.

The principal asked if I wanted to talk to her history class and speak to the school assembly the next morning, the latter of which was canceled because, Harold told me later on, someone was worried that I might say something "radical."

"This is an oil town," Harold reminded me.

I walked into the principal's class of eight seniors—mostly young men who managed to look comfortable slouched in their hard metal chairs. As the principal introduced me, I took a close look at each of the students, wondering if any of them had been part of the previous night's shooting spree.

To the class, it probably seemed as if the principal had just dragged in a bum off the highway for show-and-tell. I hadn't shaved since my trip began and hadn't showered since a Fort McMurray truck stop. Far from the swashbuckling romantic I was a week before, I now looked more like a tramp who'd steal a chicken from your backyard.

Normally, I'd be too timid to speak in front of an audience, but the hike had already instilled in me a "sure, what the hell?" attitude that made me feel carefree about pretty much anything.

I told them about my college years, my student debt, how I used to work up in Alaska, and how I lived in a van to afford grad school, but I was met with blank stares, a wall of apathy, and the realization that I was gradually becoming an Old Guy.

"Ken, do you want to tell the class why you've gone on this hike?" asked the principal, trying to steer the conversation in a more interesting direction.

"Why *am* I on this hike?" I asked myself aloud, buying myself time to dream up an answer.

Part of my reasoning was that I wanted to bring awareness to the Keystone XL and start a movement against the pipe and then grandiosely spark a revolution that would more or less bring down the entire fossil-fuel industry. But part of me wasn't exactly sure why I was out here. All I really knew was that I'd wanted to go on this hike more than anything. I guess I felt strangely drawn to the XL and the plains.

"I suppose I just wanted to go on a long walk" were the first words of my noble crusade. Sadly, they were pretty much my last, as the bell, to my relief, rang, announcing the end of the school day.

I knocked on the door at Harold's house. He wasn't home yet from school, and his pretty wife had no idea who I was, but she took my word and didn't seem at all perturbed with my giant backpack, dusty clothes, or the prospect of a complete stranger entering her house. There were eight beautiful blond children in the house, who all spoke to me with an unsettling courteousness and lack of irony. Unknown to Harold, two Mormon missionaries from Idaho had previously been invited to dinner, so it was a surprisingly large gathering for all.

I ate a plate of biscuits and a bowl of chicken potpie, always keeping my arms tight against my sides so the kids to either side of me wouldn't be bothered by any escaping odors. One of the Mormon missionaries said he'd been a rancher all his life, so I was eager to get a second opinion on my cow worries.

"Now a bull," he said, "he'll try to knock you down with his head and trample you."

"Well," I said, in need of a silver lining, "at least I don't have to worry about the female cows . . ."

"They're even worse!" he exclaimed. "Especially if you get between her and her calf. Now the bulls will run at you and close their eyes at the last second. You can get away from them. But the females, they keep their eyes open. You just better run."

I shuddered, and when our meal concluded, I accepted the family's offer to spend the night.

I took a hot shower and threw my clothes in Harold's washer, accidentally saturating a notepad I'd forgotten to remove from a pants pocket. For half an hour, I picked out sodden pieces of paper stuck to the washer's inner walls.

Harold and his wife asked if I wanted to watch a show before I went to sleep, and we watched an episode of *The Unit*, a CBS series that kicked the bucket in 2009 after four years. It was about a counterterrorism unit of commandoes who did the government's dirty work overseas. In this episode, an assassination was called off too late, and each member of the team had to find his way back home. Meanwhile, the sergeant major had problems of his own back in America when his daughter returned home from college early. I thought it was pretty tame stuff (even with an allusion to a homosexual dalliance), but in the morning, Harold felt compelled to apologize about the show, adding, "I didn't know it was going to be that . . . risqué."

That morning, Harold played the piano while his wife made me and all the kids pancakes. We all took turns reading the Book of Mormon before the kids walked to school.

This was the first time I'd ever spent more than a passing moment in a small town, and I had to admit that life never seemed so innocent and charming. After a shower, a good night's rest, a warm meal, and friendly conversation, I felt both heartwarmed by the kindness of strangers and hopeful that I could rely on the goodwill of others in the future if my body chose not to cooperate again.

I took off down the road and walked only a couple of miles, stopping to camp at the nearest cluster of trees. My feet were as bad as ever, so I took off my shoes, cleaned my wounds, generously applied creams, and sprawled out in a glade for the next twelve hours reading *The Lord of the Rings.* After a day spent walking on feet blistered and rubbed raw, I had little energy to suffer through depressing books on environmental history and energy policy, which I also had on my iPad. Rather, I looked forward to walking through fictional lands on a journey far more perilous than my own. Without the Internet or any distractions to speak of—except for maybe the groan of a distant pump jack or the nearby rustle of a deer mouse—I could read. I mean really read. Instead of checking my e-mail every half hour and falling victim to the unstoppable cycle of YouTube videos of cats falling off dressers, I'd read for hours straight. Each evening, with all this peace and silence, the stories and characters came to life.

In the early hours of the morning, there was a thick fog that settled over the prairie. Towering above the fog, sprouting from an ocean of mist, were birch trees bearing leaves on only their uppermost branches, which made them look almost tropical. The prairie, during these early mornings in Alberta, was no longer a homogenous grassland but a Jurassic savannah. A cow mooed from the fog and I imagined a brontosaur.

My feet were feeling much better. I hopped a fence and started trespassing again, following another pipeline that the Keystone XL would parallel in these parts. It was impossible to see where the pipeline had been placed in the ground, but there were roadside markers, and on the aboveground electrical wires there were big red balls indicating where the pipeline ran beneath the road, all of which, along with my compass, were useful navigational aids that kept me on a tight southeasterly course.

I walked the XL's path over prairie, occasionally coming upon an abandoned home on a gravel road overgrown with weeds and surrounded by ramshackle farming equipment that was slowly sinking into the ground. I approached one such home and yelled hello, hoping to find someone to ask for water. A dog, terrified, sprinted from the porch into the tall weeds, but I didn't hear anyone call back. With the overcast clouds, the prairie felt eerie and haunted, the land's color tinting into a dour black and white. For most of the day, I could see no roads, homes, or even planes in the sky—just a power line in the distance stretching to nowhere.

I eventually hiked to a road and ambled over to a small farm. A man on an ATV rolled up and asked what I was doing.

"I'm on a long walk," I said. "I'm headed to Texas."

"That does sound like a long walk," said the man, whose name was Carl. "Any reason why Texas?"

"Well, I'm following the proposed Keystone XL route," I said, looking behind him to see that the original Keystone pipeline, built in 2010, ran through his land.

"That pipeline there is the best thing that's ever happened to me," he said.

Before the oil company laid the pipeline in his land, Carl and several other farmers got together and persuaded the pipeline company to increase their compensation thirty times the original offer.

"It's a big boost to the local economy," he said.

I filled up a water bottle and downed it in one swift, hearty gulp. He invited me in for supper. While his wife cooked hamburgers, I asked him what the flag he had run up his flagpole represented, which was a mostly red one with a British symbol in an upper corner. He told me it was the Canadian flag used in World War II. "Then the liberals came into power in the sixties and changed it to what it is today," he said, adding with a smile, "Around here, we shoot liberals." I wasn't at all worried about getting shot by Carl, who was clearly a kind man. Rather, I felt an odd sense of comfort knowing that it's not just we Americans who casually threaten to shoot people for their political affiliation. *We're more alike than different,* I thought fuzzily.

We talked for hours about his daughters, who'd all moved to Saskatchewan; his love for flying; and the pros and cons of organic farming. "Ninety-nine percent of farmers want to be good stewards of the land," he said. "We care about the bees and bugs, and we don't like to see them go. But we have to make a living, too." He explained that pipelines are a huge part of the local and provincial economies, providing thousands of jobs and thousands of dollars in compensation for poor farmers.

Carl, to me, hardly seemed like a sellout for allowing a pipeline to cross his land. Rather, he was just a normal guy who could have used a few more bucks. Nor did any of the workers whom I'd met up in Fort McMurray strike me as "bad." They were people who, more often than not, simply wanted to provide for their families. From behind the protection of my laptop screen, it was easy to disparage those who played a part in the tar-sands economy, but now that I was breaking bread with one of them, it wasn't so easy.

Carl offered me his RV for the night, from which I listened to their golden retriever, Lou, harass prowling coyotes.

The next morning, I continued south along Highway 41, choosing not to walk through dewy fields, as I wanted to keep my feet dry while they were recovering. An illness, though, began to overtake me. The back of my throat became sore, I had a hoarse cough, and pints of green mucus gushed from my nose every hour. In an A&W bathroom the next day, I blew my nose into a sink and an adder of blood oozed out.

The next day, I broke out over prairie, and for the first time, I was caught red-handed by property owners. A man and a woman on an ATV, seeking a few sick calves in their herd, saw me and drove over. I had my map and compass in hand and my walking sticks in the crook of my arm, so I thought I at least looked like a hiker. "I'm sorry if I'm walking on your land," I said to them.

"Oh, don't worry about it," the man said with a smile. I asked him where I might find water, and he said not until the Red Deer River, which was ten miles away. He offered to go back to his house, four miles away, and get me some, but I didn't want him to go through the trouble. I said I'd make do with the liter of water I had.

I asked them what the next ten miles looked like, and they said it was all rangeland.

"You'll be fine," the husband said.

"But what will the cows do, Steve?" the wife wondered aloud.

Indeed, what will the cows do, Steve? I thought.

The husband was pensive for a moment but snapped out of it and said something reassuring.

I climbed the tallest hill with my blistered toes, swirled around on top, and didn't see one house or farm or road, only an endless rolling field of grass, the strands lazily bending with the heavier gusts of a mild breeze. The plains—except for the odd, still-standing, oil-based boomtown here and there—are mostly uninhabited, with, in some areas, one family taking care of as many as sixty thousand acres of hay fields and cattle ranges (each bigger than the city of Seattle).

There may be no finer ground to walk on than prairie. The terrain, though rolling, provides a good flat landing spot for each footfall. There are few thorns and briars, few snakes (though there are said to be rattlesnakes), few mosquitoes (at least at this time of year), and neither swamp nor talus slope to slow one's pace. Apart from the rare cactus plant (hardly bigger than a compact disc) and the mysterious and potentially leg-breaking "prairie hole" (which are gopher holes that hungry badgers have widened to about a foot in diameter), I could not ask for better ground to walk on.

I walked until I reached the Red Deer River, a sluggish river that was wide and ultimately uncrossable. I knew there was no way I could walk or swim across it with my gear, so I took a long detour off my pipeline path to walk over a bridge near the town of Bindloss, several miles to the east.

The sand hills came out of nowhere. One second I was walking over prairie, startling a pair of coyotes; the next, I was walking amid a hidden wonder of the world.

The Sand Hills are steep furry pyramids of grass that glow pink red in the dusk light. They are round, bulbous gumdrops, geographic Napoleon hats. Imagine yourself walking amid mountains that are not covered by rocks or trees but by thick grass. I scoured my mind for an analogy, and the best I could come up with were bare desert mountains made of sand and rock and ornery bush. But these were neither as barren nor as uninviting, and to compare these hills to anything would insinuate inferiority. These were hills of grass. A prairie mountain range. I stood looking over them in awe.

In the morning, I crossed the bridge to Bindloss, where I hoped to fill up with water before the long trek ahead of me over desolate country.

The town looked battered, a ghost town yet to be abandoned, the paint peeling off homes from decades of brutal, unflagging winds. It was the sort of half-deserted prairie village where you'd think it likely to hear a child's ghostly laughter coming from the abandoned school's creaky swing set. The school was boarded up, and several homes were in disrepair. When I asked a municipal worker where I could find water, he said, "This isn't a good town to get water. It's bad water here." He gave me a bottle of water and suggested I go knocking on doors to fill up the rest of my bottles.

In truth, struggling Bindloss was probably a better example of small-town North America than quaint Consort. The plains states have lost a third of their population since the population peak in the 1920s. While in some counties there has been a surge in population due to the recent fracking boom, by 1998 46 of North Dakota's 53 counties had lost population, 35 of them having so few people that they qualified as "frontier" counties. There are 6,000 ghost towns in

Kansas alone. Between 1980 and 2010, half of all rural counties in the United States decreased in population, with an especially pronounced decline in the Great Plains, where 86 percent of rural counties lost population. In these rural parts of the plains, there are only 4.2 people per square mile.

A lot of the decline has to do with technological enhancements in farming. With high-tech machines, farmers can work far more ground than their fathers could. Young people go off to college and never come back, the railroad is pulled out, the Catholic priest leaves, a bank closes, then the pool hall, then the motel, then the newspaper, and then the Main Street shops get boarded up. If the town is lucky, there'll still be a gas station that functions as a convenience store and diner.

The oil industry or a pipeline—anything that will bring in money and help keep a small town alive—is more than likely to be welcomed by these communities, whose inhabitants are aware that their town is approaching its expiration date. For them, questioning the oil industry could be the same thing as questioning their community's existence.

After knocking on a few doors, I found a man who let me fill up my bottles from a giant plastic jug of water. When I told him where I'd started my walk and where I was ending, he said, "So you're following the TransCanada pipeline, are you? Are you one of them environmentalists?"

There was something disturbing about the question. It implied—and rightly so—that there are people who care about the environment and there are people who don't. He asked the question as if I identified with some freakish sexuality. *So are you one of them erotic-vomiting quicksand fetishists?*

How could a person *not* be an environmentalist? I grew up in a suburb outside of Niagara Falls, New York, just four miles from the ghost town of Love Canal, the site of one of the most tragic environmental disasters in U.S. history. Growing up near Love Canal—where, in the 1940s, a chemical company had buried tons of toxic waste beneath a community that would, decades later, experience abnormally high cancer rates and birth defects—taught me early on what happens when industry gets to act "naturally." Wherever I went—Mississippi, Alaska, North Carolina—it seemed the captains of industry were mobilizing their forces.

There was nothing unusual about my upbringing. In North America, we all have our own Love Canals on the edge of our towns. So it was strange to me that even though the environment has been *losing* for hundreds of years, environmentalism—a term that describes simply caring about the environment—is seen as some extremist ideology. It's sad to say, but many people, perhaps like this guy, don't have the luxury of caring about the environment. In a dying town such as Bindloss, storing stacks of blue-green Keystone XL pipes (a heap of which were stacked across the road behind a cage fence) could be the town's only chance at survival. That's not to say that their amorality on the health of the environment is okay, but it does at least make their contemptuous position comprehensible.

Yes, I'm an environmentalist! I care about the fucking planet! I should have proudly announced. Instead, I sheepishly muttered something about wanting to be on a long walk, which was true, too.

With my water bottles filled, I walked out of the village, hopped a barbed-wire fence for the thirtieth time that day, and dragged my poor feet across another endless field beneath a curdled gloom-gray sky.

8.

The Ogre and the Leprechaun

October 11, 2012

←→

I hiked over pasture until reaching the Middle Sand Hills, another mountain range of grass divided by the Saskatchewan River, a wide gulp of water moseying east as slow as an arctic glacier. It had been raining all day, and the cool drops had worked together to sneak through and around my rain gear, soaking me to the bone. I happened upon an empty campground by the roadside, where, under a pavilion, I laid out all of my sopping wet clothes on a picnic table. Once in my thermal underwear, I crawled into my sleeping bag to get warm.

In the morning, I put on my still-soggy clothes, crossed the border into Saskatchewan—Saskatchewan! My first border crossing!—and picked up my next box of food at a post office and grocery store (quaintly called a "confectionary") in the town of Richmound.

Though it had been only a few weeks, it felt as if I hadn't seen a young woman in ages, so when I entered the confectionary to see a blonde-haired beauty in her early twenties, who had slender milkmaid arms and a pale complexion made ruddy by the sun, I was something close to awestruck. Abandoning all pretensions of chivalry, I leered at her from behind the pastry shelf the way a man might take a hearty swig of water before continuing his march over a desert. I tried to think of something charming to say, but the best that came out was an oafish "So what do you do for fun around here?" She was clearly uninterested in me and my trip, so I escaped the confectionary with my pride wounded and dignity barely intact.

I walked toward the town of Burstall, dubbed the "turboexpander capital of the world." (A turboexpander is a turbinelike machine that cools natural gas, and Burstall has several natural-gas pipelines leading to its expander.) There was a large, steely, pipe-cluttered industrial facility with three towering pillars spouting flames of dark-red fire. As I got closer, I figured the place would be bustling with laborers, but it was completely empty. I was within eyeshot of the compound for almost two hours, yet I saw only one truck go through.

I took a quick detour into town, where I hoped to fill my water bottles and catch up on e-mails. I entered the town bar, where a hanging bulb illuminated a lonely pool table. Pictures of Major League Baseball players hung on the walls. The only person in there was an old man sitting at a slot machine.

For the duration of my trip, I'd been updating my blog (regrettably renamed "Pipe Dreams") once or twice a week with the help of my iPad and Wi-Fi at town libraries and bars. As a blogger, I never had much of a following, but my mom and dad were avid readers, so it was only a matter of time before some of the more unsavory aspects of my adventure would come under my mother's scrutinizing eye. I opened her e-mails with as much fear and hesitation as I would opening a box full of rattlesnakes.

To: Ken Ilgunas

From: Sistine Ilgunas

Date: October 2, 2012

Subject: Re: Hi

Hi Ken,

I read your latest blog and feel I must say something. Im not going to lecture you because it doesn't work and you are an adult.

Are you not concerned about your health and safety? I find some of your escapades troubling.

Your health should not be taken for granted. The water you are drinking can be tainted as you have read in others messages to you. GI disturbances are indications that something is not right. It is also not normal to have green mucus and blood coming out of your nose. It is usually an indication of infection and a need for medication. If you get a fever and become delirious you will be in deep trouble cause no one will be there to help you. Your feet are another concern.

Your trust of strangers is another concern. Someday you will be in a situation that you are going to need help and it might not be there. I really don't know what to say anymore. I think of you every day and worry for your safety and health. Good luck to you.

Mom

To: Sistine Ilgunas

From: Ken Ilgunas

Date: October 11, 2012

Subject: Re: Hi

Oh goodness. Please understand that my every trial and challenge is magnified for dramatic effect. [This was true, but I was also censoring out stuff for my mother's benefit, such as the shooting gallery incident a week before.] I've had lots of runny noses before, so I understand how mucus works. The cold I had, anyway, is mostly long gone. And my feet are recovering. I've done 3 days of 20+miles with little soreness. And the blood was simply from a bloody nose—I've gotten a few them, largely because of the extreme dryness of the area. You shouldn't worry. I'm an adventurer! And I'm gooing through like the two safest countries in the world . . . It's not like I'm joining a band of banditos in Colombia. . . . On another note, I just crossed the Saskatchewan border. I'll have a blog post up soon, but maybe you shouldn't read the blog anymore, or else you'll worry.

Ken

My e-mail wasn't exactly truthful. My body was gradually falling apart, the temperature was getting colder, and soon I'd be traversing across America's middle section: the country's reddest, most conservative, most gun-lovingest states. I was worried, too.

But I was approaching thirty years old, and I'd long been beyond the age when my decisions could be strongly influenced by anyone, including my parents. But the reminder that other people might suffer from my being gruesomely trampled by a large ungulate did have the effect of reminding me not to do something too stupid. Yet this reminder—this chronic sense of guilt, rather—didn't really need reinforcement. In my high school years, every time I'd come home late on weekends, my mother would come down the stairs in her nightgown and stick her nose in my mouth like a mother bird about to lovingly regurgitate food into her offspring's gullet, except that she was merely interested in determining, all while carrying the air of some wise olfactory connoisseur, whether or not I'd been drinking or smoking pot. I didn't do either of those things, as I spent most of my late teenage years playing video games with friends. But she always convinced herself that she smelled something incriminating. She'd take a step back and look at her depraved son with a mix of anger and disappointment. I'd break out into nervous giggles at the absurdity of the whole demonstration, which was further confirmation to her that I'd been smoking the Bobo bush.

"Yeah, keep laughing," she'd say. "You're going to get yourself killed one of these days. You'll see."

To: Ken Ilgunas

From: Sistine Ilgunas

Date: October 11, 2012

Subject: Re: Hi

Thank god u r ok. Yes maybe I should stop reading it.

Mom xo

I also had a heckler (Hey, Dennis!) who for the last several years had been sending me an almost daily blog comment in which he'd question my sexuality, or call me stupid or a "libtard." Normally, I was relieved to see his comments because they were confirmation that someone was actually reading my stuff, but now that I had all the time in the world to think, I found myself dwelling for hours on his ungrammatical barbs. "God , you really love yourself. no wonder you dont have a steady boyfriend," he wrote, followed by, "Its fun to watch you libs do your circle jerk , hahaha." Another comment read: "ur just lazy and like to travel. lots of people do that. i know , i'm one of them . But i dont go around masquerading as some hobo philosophiser , :)))))."

There was sometimes an ounce of truth to the comments, which made them linger longer than I would have liked, but I was able to put them out of my mind when I saw an e-mail with the subject heading "CBC Request" pop up in my in-box.

To: Ken Ilgunas

From: Marian Mew

Date: October 11, 2012

Subject: CBC Request

Hi Ken,

I am a producer with CBC TV. I just heard about your walk from Hardisty to Houston.

We'll be out in Saskatchewan early next week and I am wondering if there is any chance we can hook up with you on Tuesday Oct. 16.

Please contact me via email or my cell 403-xxx-xxxx.

Looking forward to hearing from you.

marian

Marian Mew

Producer, CBC Television

403-xxx-xxxx (b)

403-xxx-xxxx (c)

xxxxxxxxx@cbc.ca

The CBC! I knew from living near the Canadian border as a boy and getting Canadian TV stations that the CBC was a major Canadian television network. How did they find my little blog? In any case, I wondered if this was my opportunity to use my "voice." I e-mailed them and told them they could meet me in a few days in Val Marie, a town in Saskatchewan just north of the Montana border.

Meanwhile, in Burstall, I ordered a Macho Burger with fries. Four workers ambled into the bar for their afternoon lunch break. They were all in their forties, except one guy my age who was clearly upset about something. He sank into his chair, put his elbows up on the table, and held his head in his hands. The older guys tried to cheer him up.

"That's Babe Ruth," one guy said to the young man, pointing to a picture on the wall. "And he was a fucking orphan!"

It turned out that the young man was having lady problems. I wasn't sure what Babe Ruth had to do with that, but I admired the group's attempt to support their young friend. The gruffest of the four men, a short but stout worker of Irish descent, who called himself the Leprechaun, looked me up and down, his face lighting up with an expression of amused confusion, as if he'd just happened upon some mysterious ribbon-wrapped present.

"Hey man," he barked. "What are you doing here with that backpack?"

I said I was walking to Texas.

After the standard diagnoses of "You're crazy" that I'd already gotten used to, the younger guy perked up and asked, "Was that you on the highway? I thought you were a native vagrant."

The boys tilted their heads back and unleashed wild, breathy, emphysemic laughter.

The Leprechaun asked me why I was hiking. I said I thought it might give me something to write about.

"We got a writer here," he mockingly called out to the bar.

"This feller here," said the Leprechaun, pointing to his friend, whom he called the Ogre. "This feller here, he's been drinking since he was ten! Ten! Put that in your fucking book!"

"I'm not sure if that's going to make it into my book," I said politely, feeling for the Ogre, who seemed far more mild mannered than the rest of the gang. (At this point, I had no intention of turning my hike into a book, but I'd already learned that my motivations made more sense to people if I could tell them I went on the trip for reasons of work rather than "the yearnings of my soul.")

Every minute, the Leprechaun would say something funny to his trio of friends, then look over at me, and say, "Put that in your fucking book!" which was followed by laughter from all around the table. As they guzzled more Labatt Blues, the camaraderie of the group was growing more violent by the second. I began nervously eyeing the bar for the nearest pool cue and wondering whom I should incapacitate first.

"I got beat up in a bar by two drunks," the Leprechaun yelled. "Put that in your book, too!"

The waitress gave the Leprechaun a disgusted look while strangling the tops of three empty beer bottles to lift them off the table.

"I'm just playing with you, man," said the Leprechaun consolingly. "I gotta do that to my friends. You're in the circle now."

He came over and whipped a ten-dollar bill at me, which floated down onto my keyboard.

"Be careful out there," he said. "Watch out for the ghosts. The Ogre and the Leprechaun."

I walked south as quickly as I could, determined to get through Saskatchewan, Montana, and South Dakota—the places where I thought it might get unmanageably cold. I leaped over latitudinal hurdles with gusto, hoping that when winter arrived I'd be in the relatively warmer climes of Nebraska, Kansas, Oklahoma, and Texas.

I'd been moving fast, with several twenty-mile days under my belt. The chafing on my toes had mostly healed, and while there was one lingering blister, my feet were no longer the problem they once were. I did, though, begin to develop new chafing, this time around my heels, which was uncomfortable, but the variety of antifungal creams I generously spread over them seemed to be bringing a halt to the fungus's expansion.

For these last few days, I'd had a nice clear path. Another pipeline, called the Vantage Pipeline, which would transport ethane from North Dakota to Alberta and would, for some time, parallel the path of the XL, was being laid into the ground. So I had a dirt path to follow for days, allowing me to stuff my compass in my pocket and focus entirely on putting one foot in front of the other.

But that didn't stop me from having to walk through cow herds— my biggest anxiety. Up until now, I'd been walking about half the time over hay and wheat fields, and the other half through cow pasture. Of the various terrains, the pastures were easily the most scenic and foot friendly. They're huge and often barren of roads and all other signs of mankind except a few barbed-wire fences separating ranchers' herds. Normally, I'd walk through the pastures without even seeing a cow.

Sometimes, because of the cows, I'd go on long detours to avoid having to push through a herd. But when there were hundreds of them and no alternate routes, I had no choice but to advance into the thick of them.

In the field ahead, black cows were bunched together in a tight herd, calmly plucking mouthfuls of dry grass with heads lowered. Without any other path, I walked straight toward the herd. As I approached, one lifted its head from the grass, a few strands still sticking out the side of his mouth. It went completely still and stared at me. After a few moments, all forty or so cows stopped grazing and, similarly captivated, watched me and my swinging trekking poles steadily advance.

One, unsure about me, took off on a sprint away from me, and the whole herd all at once stormed away in the same direction. I felt as if I were an encroaching legion of Viking warriors that caused villagers to rush from homes in a panicked stampede. Just by walking toward them, my meager 180-pound body scared away upward of 40,000 pounds of fat and muscle. This was more or less what happened every time.

I walked with long, straining strides through yet another herd. They weren't clustered in a group or off to one side as they normally were, but evenly distributed over the pasture, hundreds spread everywhere, dotting the dry green-brown grass in the same scattered way the small puffy white clouds were spread evenly across the blue sky. They were unavoidable. The only thing I could do was to get through this pasture as fast as I could in order to minimize the risk of an attack. The added quickness to my stride made my left shin tighten. After I escaped the cows and resumed my normal steady pace, the pain did not leave; rather, it grew more unbearable by the hour. Each step felt as if I were carrying a heavy cannonball in my shin. Or it felt as if my shinbone were splintering and the bone shards would soon pierce my skin. Or it felt as if, any step now, my shinbone would break in two and I'd have to drag a dangling leg over the prairie. I couldn't take the pain anymore, so I dropped my stuff at the first tree I saw and set up my tent in the middle of cow country next to a thin creek that a beaver had logged, creating a foggy swamp above the creek. Throughout the night, the beaver would slam its tail on the swamp's misty surface, startling me wide awake. I looked carefully at my shin, and I couldn't tell what had been causing the pain.

Lying in my sleeping bag, I envisioned a cow rolling over onto my tent, which would, of course, cause my head to rocket off and my guts to neatly squeeze out of my neck like toothpaste. Upon turning off my iPad after an evening of reading, I thought I'd begun to understand why Tolkien created Sauron's "eye"—the big, flaming, omnipotent eye set atop a pillar in Mordor that looked over everything. The hobbits often felt the eye looking over them even when they were not within its immediate line of sight. For this first leg of my trip, I felt as if there were something constantly glaring down at me, making me uneasy and edgy. The eye, I realized, was fear. Fear of getting caught. Fear of getting shot. Fear of getting trampled. Fear of not finishing. Fear of everything. It wasn't something that felt as if it came from inside of me; rather, it came from someplace else, like an evil spirit, a dream-invading succubus, a ghost that won't leave the attic. Chronic fear, I recognized, is a horrible thing to have to live with, and I began wondering if all those people living adventureless lives, serenely watching TVs in their bedrooms, knew something I didn't.

When I awoke and packed up my tent, I noted that my shin was far worse. I was now walking with an undeniable limp. When I got going, I was able to maintain a sluggish pace for a while, but when I stopped to take a break, it was agonizing to get back up on my feet.

I scanned my map and decided to aim for the nearest town: Shaunavon, Saskatchewan, where I hoped to find a warm place to recover. An old man in his truck saw me limping down the road and using my trekking poles to keep from placing too much pressure on my leg. He asked if I wanted a lift, and I almost shed a tear when I declined—both proud of my resolve to walk every step of the way and disgraced by my pitiful condition.

It's frustrating when every piece of you—mind, body, and soul—wishes to go on but can't because one small part of you doesn't want to. I'd already begun to think of my body less as "me" and more as a shell, a machine, or a vehicle that carried me. My arms and legs weren't "me." When I cursed my shin or foot, I might as well have been cursing a blown tire or a dead battery in my van.

Yet, despite my physical degradation, I couldn't help but be mesmerized by the human body. The body does so much without any sort of guidance or conscious thought. At night, while I read or slept, it was busy digesting food, sealing up the cold sore on my lip, clearing the chafing on my heels, reducing the inflammation in my shin, soothing the dark bruises on my hips. You don't need to tell the body to do any of these things; it does them automatically and usually quite well. Even conscious movements became more and more unconscious. I wouldn't have to think to put my leg forward; I just walked, unconsciously throwing one foot in front of the other until I felt some overriding compulsion to sit down and rest. Soon, the swing of my trekking poles became automatic, too, as would scanning the terrain for helpful topographical features, watering holes, and homes. As my body took on all these jobs and began to perform them without any conscious direction, I was eventually granted the much-needed peace to let my mind wander. The body, for all its complexity, sophistication, and evolutionary magnificence, is nothing but 180 pounds of machinery that exists so we can carry in our heads a few weightless dreams, ideas, and memories—what we think of as our "self."

But, for the last few days, "I" hardly got to come out, as it's impossible to enjoy a walk, let alone have the time for an idle thought, when you're in constant pain. The pain outscreams all thoughts, and the only thoughts you have are about how much pain you're in. As I made my way into the heart of Shaunavon, I tripped on a big stone, fell, gripped my shin, looked up into the sky, and screamed, *"WHY?"*

I set up my tent in the town's RV campground, which had closed for the season. The next morning, I bought a seventy-five-dollar room at the Stardust Motel, where I took a shower and proceeded to not do anything—let me rephrase: *I did nothing*—for the next sixteen hours. That is, I did nothing except lie in bed in my underwear eating a whole block of mozzarella cheese and watching a marathon of *Gilmore Girls*, all while placidly wallowing in self-pity, already too far along in the postinjury grieving process to feel something as emotionally taxing as anger. I leaned over the bed and grabbed my stick of pepperoni from the nightstand.

I couldn't justify spending more money on an expensive motel room for more than a night, so I spent the next two back at the empty RV campground, going in and out of the nearby pharmacy, where I tried to figure out how to hasten my recovery. I bought gelled shoe soles, a bottle of Ibuprofen, and an ACE bandage that I tightly wrapped around my shin. In the town library, moving my leg under the computer desk required the use of both of my arms. When I noted that I couldn't comfortably walk to the bathroom, I realized that walking the length of a whole country probably wouldn't be any easier, and I began to wonder if I'd have to soon call it quits. I gently lifted my leg and put it on the seat of the chair in front of me.

No longer with the comfort of a TV to feed my newfound *Gilmore*

Girls fixation (will Rory's school year rebound after she gets a D on her Shakespeare exam?), I spent most of my time boning up on climate change and energy policy to prepare for my CBC interview.

Like a spurned lover listening to sappy love songs, I pondered the hopelessness of environmentalism and wallowed in doomsday prophecies about our warming planet.

I knew that across the world there are more than one billion cars on the road, more than 100,000 flights a day, and roughly 7,000 active coal-fired generator units. In the U.S. alone there are 1.1 million gas and fracking wells. All of these emit astounding amounts of CO_2 into the atmosphere—now currently at over 400 parts per million—the highest CO_2 level we've had in our atmosphere in the last 400,000 years. I knew experts believe that to get a handle on climate change we must hogtie a tremendously powerful fossil-fuel industry into keeping most of the remaining fossil fuels, valued at around twenty trillion dollars, in the ground.

What is the solution? How will we get there? If we could travel five hundred years into the future and see that things turned out okay, how did we make it okay, and how can we now, as individuals and as a country, make real this future of okayness?

With a well-meaning government, some thinkers believe that we can stave off environmental collapse with innovative economic policies. The most well-known is the unsexily titled "cap and trade" policy by which the government "caps" the amount of greenhouse gases that can be emitted by coal plants and refineries and other polluters. Another idea is a carbon tax, which would make us pay more for fossil fuels and therefore give us a reason to consume less, and which has been implemented with success in British Columbia. Some state and local governments have been keen on experimenting with such ideas, yet, for the usual political reasons, they're unlikely to be instituted on the national level; and to lower emissions on a global level we need not just the full participation of one country but the whole world. Getting everyone to sign up to contend with the urgent realities of climate change seems next to impossible.

Technology offers a range of options, some more realistic than others. One of the more controversial methods is geoengineering, in which human beings attempt to alter the earth's natural systems to fend off climate change. In 2012, entrepreneur Russ George dumped 220,000 pounds of iron sulphate into the Pacific Ocean as an experiment in "iron fertilization" to encourage the growth of phytoplankton, which can jumpstart biological activity and help remove carbon dioxide from the atmosphere. Such ideas are mostly dismissed because practically everyone acknowledges that there could be a host of logistical problems and unforeseen consequences, not to mention that geoengineering does nothing to address the root of the problem.

Most everyone in the world supports the development of solar and wind energies, and two scientists from UC Davis have gone as far as to assert that we have the technology now (but not the infrastructure or political support) to fulfill all our energy needs with renewable sources. But some environmentalists aren't so optimistic. Andrew Nikiforuk, author of *The Energy of Slaves*, wonders if we're failing to appreciate just how much space is required to replace relatively compact fossil-fuel energy plants with a sprawling collection of renewable sources of energy. For example, replacing the energy created by a thousand-megawatt coal-fired plant (which covers 1.5 square miles) with solar panels would require 19 square miles—the size of a small city. Wind would take up three times the space. We tend to think of solar and wind energy as "free" energy, in that they serve no purpose in and of themselves, and that we're just wasting these natural energy flows by not harvesting them with panels and turbines. But taking from the earth's natural energy flows comes with consequences. In 2008, a group of physicists in the journal *Ecological Complexity* reminded us that the wind doesn't blow purposely; it is a participant in weather and storm activities, and wind turbines and solar panels disrupt the "natural energy flows upon which all life now depends." They estimate that the earth's natural systems are fit to supply no more than 10 percent of our power needs.

Technology, anyway, does little to address the underlying problems: overpopulation and excessive consumption. Contrary to popular wisdom, with every new "green" technology, consumption doesn't go down; it goes up or stays the same. David Owen, in his book *The Conundrum*, points out that technology makes things cheaper (a flight to London) and more efficient (a Prius), but that means we can fly more and drive more, which means the new technology will ultimately have no impact on reducing overall consumption and greenhouse-gas emissions. Between 1987 and 2002, despite improvements in lighting efficiency, Owen points out that "household energy use rose in every income category." Since the mid-1970s, refrigerators have become remarkably more efficient, but food waste has risen, and as a country, we now throw away 40 percent of all the edible food we produce.

"The world's main emitter of man-made greenhouse gases," says Owen, "has always been prosperity." This was made clear in 2009, a year after the recession, when a reduction in prosperity caused annual carbon emissions to shrink 6 percent.

Because the obstacles between us and innovative economic policies, sustainable technology, and consumption reduction appear to be insurmountable, the most sensible conclusion one could reach might be: "Wow, we're probably pretty fucked." I wondered: Why was I suffering for a pipeline that will probably be built and probably won't make all that much of a difference in a world already crisscrossed by pipelines and powered by fossil fuels?

On my fourth day in town, I slipped in my Dr. Scholl's gelled insoles, popped my first of three Ibuprofens, and tightly wrapped an ACE bandage around my lower leg. For the first time in close to a week, I could walk in relative comfort.

Relief! Hope! Ecstasy!

That was what I felt as I walked through the dim streets of Shaunavon on that clear, brisk morning.

I took off over pasture, where I was approached by three galloping horses. I rubbed my hand up and down their heads, brushing my knuckles against their soft snouts. I didn't realize until then just how much I'd craved the touch of another creature. When I came across coyotes, I'd watch remorsefully as they sprinted from me in terror. *Come back!* I'd think. *Oh, how nice it would be to have a companion on two legs or four!*

An enormous herd of mule deer, fifty strong, moved en masse like a horde of marathon runners, squeezing their formation into an orderly single-file line as they approached a barbed-wire fence, where each would have its turn jumping over the wire, diving skyward with front hooves extended, where, for just a moment, the deer appeared to be suspended in motion before gracefully arcing back down to earth and immediately getting back to the business of madly sprinting over the grass.

A badger nervously waddled away, and I caught sight of three white-bellied, dark-nosed pronghorn soaring across the prairie like comets, leaving behind them a tail of shuddering grass. In a hay field, thousands of ducks rose and circled the field like the slow rotation of clouds right before a twister touches down.

I'd gone the whole morning without coming remotely close to a house, but I saw a few buildings on my map and hoped someone lived in one. (With so many homes abandoned on the prairie, I was never sure which were inhabited and which weren't.) When I approached a house in the afternoon, I saw a woman hauling a giant bucket of water. I worried that my presence might startle her, but she reacted nonchalantly, as if bedraggled strangers in these remote parts were as common as cows moaning from the fields. She told me I could camp on her land. Her husband, Ron, offered to bring me back a plate of warm food because he and his wife were going to a fall festival dinner in the village of Climax. That night, they invited me in, and I ate a meal of corn, turkey, potatoes, stuffing, and a slice of cherry cream-cheese pie.

Ron told me about how he'd been a farmer all his life, as had his son, who lived next door. Ron was in his late seventies and had had several types of cancer. When he complained about pains to his doctor, the doctor said, "You're getting old. I can't give you a pill to make you younger."

"When you get old, they're not as willing to spend lots of money on you," Ron said, smiling.

He took a flight to Tijuana, Mexico, where he received some unorthodox medical treatment and dietary instructions on how to eat healthier, cutting from his diet processed sugar, white flour, and pork. He recovered and has been healthy ever since. I asked him if he still supports socialized medicine, and he said, "You betcha." Despite almost dying, he believed that the system was good for the many even if it hurt the few.

The next day, I continued on over the prairie. I came across a herd of cows, and feeling an odd sense of composure, I walked right through the middle of their ranks, dividing the anxious herd as if I were parting the Red Sea. Fear, it seems, is something that isn't quite conquered but gradually forgotten.

My shin was still sore, but I was able to maintain a steady stride despite the fresh gashes spreading across my heels and a blister emerging on my broken little toe. I staggered into Val Marie in the late afternoon. The gravel roads led to two granaries near the middle of town. The paint on the antichoice signs put up by the Knights of Columbus had mostly peeled off.

I stopped in the town's hotel/restaurant to buy some juice. When I went to leave to find a campsite, the owner stopped me and offered a room. "I'm afraid that's not in my budget," I said to her.

"It's on me," she said.

It was just a small room with an aged bathtub, but for a sore, weary traveler, it was a royal gift for which I was deeply, inexpressibly grateful.

On this trip, the locals had every reason to keep their distance and be suspicious, and even treat me with a sort of guarded contempt. Yet they had shown me nothing but compassion and generosity, opening their hearts and doors to this dusty, bearded, limping backpacker who could conceivably be a criminal.

It's easy for an independent and self-reliant person who rarely, if ever, needs help from strangers to lose sight of the better angels of our nature. That's the price we pay when we strive to become immune to vulnerability, as I suppose we all should. After just a few weeks of travel, my cynicism, which I'd once considered a central and rather unbecoming personal characteristic, was breaking apart and dissipating like one of these prairie clouds after a thundershower.

To travel alone, I'd learned, isn't to rely on yourself. To travel alone is to force yourself to depend on others. It is to fall in love with mankind.

9.

The Posse

October 20, 2012

←→

In Val Marie, a reporter, producer, and cameraman from CBC's show *The National* stopped by to talk with me.

It was surreal watching my little journey—which I'd told practically no one about until just a few weeks before I'd set out—getting attention from a major national news network.

We walked around town while I pretended to tie my boot laces, get my package from the post office, and hop over a barbed-wire fence.

The reporter asked me something along the lines of "How have your views changed on the XL during the course of your trip?" I didn't want to come across as an environmental lunatic, which would automatically get me dismissed by at least half the viewing public, so I played down the whole "y'all are goin' to hell" sentiment and instead tried to come across as something more culturally acceptable—"a young man on a journey."

"To go on a journey," I said, "is to be changed by the experiences you have and the people you meet and the places you see. [When you] go into a journey with some sort of rigid stance, you're kind of closing yourself off from those opportunities."

I believed in all that, but when I watched the interview later on, I felt disgusted with myself for squandering an opportunity to say something true and useful, choosing instead to timidly utter what can aptly be called "uncontroversial bullshit."

I explained why this hike couldn't be an anti-oil protest since all my gear, clothes, and food either had been created by petroleum or was shipped using it or contained the product itself. The reporter then asked, "Do you think that's why they're building this pipeline?" (In other words, "Do you think we need oil?") I felt as if I had a response deep in the recesses of my mind, but I stumbled and stammered and scolded myself for the rest of the day.

There are times when the wind, unimpeded by forest or mountain, blows over the plains with the force of a buffalo stampede. It isn't a series of gusts like it is in most places, but a constant heavy current that rushes against you without diminishment. It's as if you've positioned your squinty-eyed, hair-tossed head directly in front of the earth's air conditioner.

That night, I tried to set up my tent on the open prairie, but rocking waves of wind sweeping over the land gathered up and threw my loose items—tent bags and sleeping pad—over the grass, sending me on a series of mad dashes to retrieve them.

After collecting my things, I tried to plant my feet on the corners of my fluttering tent, which dodged my every move like a cursed Twister mat. Realizing I'd never get the tent up and that it wouldn't stay upright even if I could set it up, I repacked my stuff and walked to a nearby road. I set the tent up in a ditch alongside the road, where there was enough protection from the wind. But around two a.m., the wind shifted direction, attacking my tent from the exposed side. The walls of my tent flapped deafeningly, sounding like the noisy crescendo just before a nerve-racking rocket launch. The wind was so loud I was compelled to unzip the door and poke my head out to see if there was an approaching tornado.

The wind yanked one of the tent stakes from the ground and launched it into the tall grass. (I had just four stakes, so losing one was a bit of a big deal.) My tiny tent collapsed on me, and one of my trekking poles was beating against my chest. I was frantically trying to stop the pole from hitting me, searching for the tent zipper, and squealing through my first taste of claustrophobia.

I got out, turned my headlamp on, and walked the road in search of large rocks (of which, apparently, there are very few on this part of the prairie) so I could hold the tent in place with their weight.

In the morning, groggy eyed and with a disgraceful mop of bed head, I dismantled the tent, and a man, whom I'd met the previous day, slowed down and screamed out from his driver's-side window, "I like my truck!" before speeding off back to Val Marie.

The wind picked up. At times, I felt as if I could lean forward and the wind would hold me still. The tumbleweeds did not tumble across the prairie; they hovered several feet in the air, crashing into a barbed-wire fence, where hundreds crowded together desperately gripping the wire or one another. The ferocious winds turned the prairie grass into a field of flames, lifting and falling, lifting and falling, dancing and licking and lifting and falling. Above me, the clouds fast-forwarded across the sky.

Unobscured by buildings, hillsides, or trees, the plains' sky is huge, blooming open from horizon to horizon, colored with a light pastel blue on its petal's farthest horizon edge that deepens into a rich dark blue directly overhead until it becomes a blinding yellow pollen at its bright center.

How can one describe the immensity of the plains' sky? You could say you can rotate your body in a 360-degree swirl and always see the sky, and that's true. You could say you can look forward, look above you, and even tilt your head all the way back to your heels and take in the sky in one full, albeit awkward, motion. And that's true, too. But there's no way you can ever fully take in a plains' sky. It's just too big. It's impossible to capture with a camera lens, let alone a pair of eyes. You look at the sky one moment, tie your bootlaces the next, and look up again and see something completely new, with new shapes and positions of clouds, a new slant of sunlight. Sometimes the moment-to-moment change is stark. Sometimes it's subtle. But there is always ongoing change, a constant newness, a never-before-seen and never-to-be-re-created composition of color, cloud, and prairie dust that will force its sightseers to concede that the plains are far from a land of unvarying monotony. It is most magnificent after an evening rainstorm when the clouds break apart and the sky becomes a watering hole for an ecosystem of cloud species, each its own shape and shade, with its own interests and intentions.

Behind me were smoky blue-gray plumes, as if a city just beyond the horizon had been set ablaze. Directly to the left was a long, thin, curved cloud, a horizontal scabbard, frayed at the edges. To my front left, far in the distance along the horizon, was a mountain chain of clouds, their snow-topped crests a rosy evening pink. Directly in front of me was an upside-down atom bomb explosion, with a wide bottom and a cylinder of smooth and unruffled whiteness rising above it. Here and there were your standard white puffy clouds, small and compact, solitary buffalo taking a break from the herd to graze alone in the dark-blue grass. To my front right was a big bulbous heap of white clouds, a pyramid of popcorn that sat in front of a dark-gray storm farther back, way back, that was sending down sheets of dark rain. Directly above me was a drab gray that belched a gentle thunder. Straight to my right, to the west, with the sun easing its way down, was the most spectacular cloud collection yet: the sun sending shafts of light through pillows of cottony clouds, tearing them apart into an explosion of feathers. The torn clouds were a gloomy gray on one side and a resplendent white where their frothy edges met the full force of the sun.

I felt as if I were carrying this great blue dome above me, a Sistine ceiling, a vast ever-changing sky painting: schools of drifting clouds; flecks of sparkling star light; Serengetis of chirping, squeaking, honking birds; wildernesses of insects; the sun rising to its bleary afternoon heights or sinking down for sleep beneath purple-red clouds. It is a vast inverted ocean that is—because it has, when you think about it, no true border, no real extent, no absolute limit—infinite.

I crossed the border into Montana. America. Home. "No Trespassing" country.

No one in Canada had a problem with my trespassing over their property, but someone in nearly every Montana town I passed through would inform me with morbid certainty that I was crazy. And then they'd warn me (in a friendly sort of way) that I'd get shot for trespassing on so-and-so's land. People who didn't even own land would tell me not to trespass.

No trespassing and private property signs are posted on trees and fence posts all across rural America. Even where there aren't signs, Americans simply don't have the freedom (or implicit permission) to saunter through their town's neighboring woods and fields. In the Piedmont region of rural North Carolina, where I'd been living off and on for the past few years, almost every home had no trespassing signs posted on trees, barring walkers from acres and acres of woodland. If you talk to an American about this, he'll say, "Tough luck," as if this tradition of exclusion were the natural state of things.

But trespassing is a bizarre concept in other countries. Continental European countries such as Germany, Denmark, and Switzerland allow hikers to roam forests, unenclosed land, and alpine pastures even though these places aren't designated national parks. Scandinavian countries, by law, give access to virtually the whole countryside, permitting campfires, camping, swimming, berry gathering, and, of course, hiking. You can walk across virtually any countryside you care to. In Finland, it's called *jokamiehenoikeus*. In Scotland, it's "the right to roam." In Sweden, it's *allemansrätt* (or "every man's right"). In Sweden (and I love this), fences put up for the sole purpose of keeping people out must be torn down, and property owners are actually prohibited from posting NO TRESPASSING signs (unless they're there to keep walkers out of a sensitive area). It's not a free-for-all for hikers, by any means. Hikers are required to stay at least sixty-five yards from homes and could be sentenced to as much as four years in jail for destroying property. *Allemansrätt* is friendly to landowners because landowners can't be sued by hikers if the hiker has an accident on the landowner's property. In the U.S., landowners who let people run wild on their land run the risk of being sued, so their NO TRESPASSING sign is often not just an ornery message but a kind of legal suit of armor.

For all the signs that threaten the would-be trespasser, cases in which trespassers have been shot are rare but not unheard of. In 2009, a family in Liberty County, Texas, was driving home from an evening of swimming. When they parked on the side of the road to pee in the woods, they were met with gunfire from nearby homeowners who'd crafted a sign that read TRESPASSERS WILL BE SHOT. SURVIVORS WILL BE RE SHOT!! SMILE I WILL. The four family members were shot with a twelve-gauge shotgun, including a seven-year-old boy who was hit in the head and died.

Perhaps the most well-known trespassing tragedy is the case of Yoshihiro Hattori, a Japanese exchange student in Louisiana. In 1992, Hattori, who'd dressed for a Halloween party as John Travolta from *Saturday Night Fever*, accidentally approached the wrong house and was shot by homeowner Rodney Peairs. The event sparked an international relations nightmare.

Such a violent reaction to a person's walking across someone's property was bewildering to me because—even though I was breaking the law—I'd never once felt like I was doing anything wrong. Walking cross-country is like crocheting or picking berries: It's so harmless and innocent that you begin to feel harmless and innocent, too. You feel *wholesome*.

Why are we like this? Why are we so obsessed with private property?

Our systems of property derive largely from our English legal ancestry. English Puritans who settled in Massachusetts understood private property to be "akin to the right to absolute possession of [a man's] own soul and conscience," writes author Richard Slotkin. But unlike England, America doesn't have much of a history of the "commons," where English villagers, for centuries, shared land for grazing cattle, collecting firewood, and other practical purposes. America was, from the beginning, a private property country.

By the mid-eighteenth century, most colonists owned land and 80 percent of the population worked in agriculture. Thomas Jefferson believed that property rights gave citizens economic security and a sense of self-reliance, which he thought would encourage independent political judgment. (Jefferson, understandably, didn't foresee conservative talk radio.) He imagined a nation of farmers, and his vision would influence federal land-distribution polices.

With the passage of the Land Ordinance of 1785, Congress set out to survey land to the west of the established states, dividing up the still-undeveloped continent into square 640-acre sections. "The national grid," John Hanson Mitchell writes in his book *Trespassing*, "was essentially the ultimate expression of private property . . . [America] viewed land not as a place of wildness and beauty or a source of sustenance but above all as a commodity to be bought and sold primarily for capital gain."

The U.S. military waged war with the Plains Indians throughout the 1860s and 1870s, pushing them off their ancestral lands and making the settling of the West inevitable. In the 1880s, the lines on the map became lines on the ground with the advent of barbed wire. Without cheap mass-produced barbed wire, it would have been impossible to successfully subdivide the plains (where there weren't enough trees to build long wooden fences). Land that had been borderless from the dawn of time was suddenly a checkerboard of wire.

Over time, the idea of "no trespassing" became legally sanctioned.

The Supreme Court acknowledged that in areas where there is a "common understanding" the public is permitted to hunt, fish, and travel over private land, but this right is revoked the second a landowner posts a NO TRESPASSING sign or builds a fence. This is referred to as the "power to exclude," and it's given to all property owners.

Consequently, going for a long walk on the plains is impossible unless you are an owner of a large piece of property or if you have obliging property-owning neighbors. Barbed-wire fences, NO TRESPASSING signs, legal impediments, and a general feeling of unwelcomeness, not to mention the fear of getting shot, make travel over huge swaths of the country—and by no means just the Great Plains—difficult, illegal, and practically impossible.

In America, the so-called freest country on Earth, no one really has the right to roam. To walk across wild America, except in national parks and on government-approved trails, you have no choice but to trespass.

A sorry state of sauntering, indeed.

"Don't you think it's a little late in the year to be traveling?" asked the cashier at the Reynolds Market in Glasgow, Montana, pop. 3,253. Sliding a box of Pop-Tarts and a stack of jumbo-size candy bars over the scanner, the cashier, an old woman who I sensed was the type who normally radiated a grandmotherly warmth, asked her question with a steely coldness. This was not the innocent query of a stranger but the stern admonishment of a mother, one who keenly and quickly gathered the foolishness of my enterprise and who spoke to me as if I were a member of her brood.

I felt embarrassed and guilty and tried to reassure her—but was really trying to reassure myself—that I wouldn't have to deal with the Montana cold (which, in December, gets down to an average of seven degrees Fahrenheit) since I was heading south to warmer climes, far from the icy clutches of a Montana winter. The clerk shook her head and warned me to at least stay away from the town of Wolf Point. "If anyone there as much as walks toward you, get away," she said. Not too long before, a forty-three-year-old female teacher was abducted and killed by two men who worked in the nearby oil boomtowns.

"And don't shoot yourself," she said, with just the slightest touch of humor.

Her last piece of advice was in reference to a little Glasgow inside joke I'd heard a few times already, alluding to an incident that took place in town a few months before my visit. Ray Dolin, a struggling thirty-nine-year-old photographer from West Virginia, was hitchhiking across the country to write a photographic memoir called *Kindness in America*. Dolin took a bus to Montana, where he began his hitchhike, but was promptly shot in the arm by a stranger in a passing car outside of Glasgow. Naturally, the people of Glasgow were ashamed that one of their own would do such a thing. But, in the months that followed, after the police had arrested a potential shooter, Dolin confessed that he'd actually shot himself, claiming that he was trying to commit suicide. For good reason, the authorities were unconvinced, suspecting that Dolin's misfire was actually a bold and rather bloody publicity stunt for his memoir.

Dolin was the talk of the town, and wherever I went in Glasgow, people flashed a relieved smile, and said something along the lines of "You're not going to shoot yourself while you're here, are you?"

I continued on over cow pastures, hay fields, and country roads. I slept next to a church in the town of Whitewater, was followed by two snarling curs near a farmer's home, and usually sought a home once a day where I might fill up my water bottles. All my foot problems began to gradually disappear. They were getting tougher, but I'd also become far more fastidious about my foot care. Each night, I'd clean them rigorously, scrubbing in between my toes, clipping my toenails, applying creams, and adjusting Band-Aids. I began to appreciate why there are religious foot-washing rituals, which I used to think were yet more bizarre and kinky religious ceremonies. But I realized that feet, on a walk especially, ought to be washed with great care. They ought to be washed *religiously*. When my feet were useless, I was useless.

As for my shin splints, usually I'd start the day with a hardly perceptible soreness, making me wonder if my shin had fully healed up overnight. But halfway through the day, I'd awkwardly step on a rock, or sink my foot into a gopher hole, or get it tangled in soybean vines, and I'd fall to the ground in agony, look up into the sky with moist eyes, and cry out, *"WHY?"*

The deeper into Montana I hiked, the more the landscape changed. The grassy prairie became grayer and rockier. These hills—replete with fossils and dinosaur bones—seemed old, dry, decaying. The place was a geological sideshow: giant slabs precipitously balanced atop thin columns of dirt; the ground sinking an inch with each footfall as if it were full of air; the rocks so soft they'd shatter when I tried to use them to hammer in my tent stakes. The rotting, flaky cliffs were like statues, worn and crumbling, reminders of a grander age. I had the impression that mighty things happened here long ago. Now, the land's denizens—farmers and hunters and livestock—

seemed to be mere tourists on a historic battlefield where Jurassic glories once shook the earth.

As I walked from Glasgow to Nashua, the temperature chilled and the wind picked up, seeping through layers and biting my skin with frosty fangs. I put on my hat and gloves. Then my coat. Then my raincoat and pants. And finally, at night, my thermal underwear. In my tent, in all my clothes, in my five-degrees-Fahrenheit-rated sleeping bag, I still couldn't stop shivering. This was troubling because I was wearing every article of clothing I had with me, and if it had been another ten or twenty degrees colder, I would have suffered all the more.

I came across my first Keystone XL workers—twentysomethings in a pickup truck doing surveying work—who seemed happy to meet me. Their older, gruffer overseer told me that I wasn't allowed to trespass, and when I politely told him I'd been doing just that for more than a month, he scoffed and drove off. Another middle-aged guy, this one a local with a cowboy hat and a long beard with no mustache, told me, in a kinder way, to stick to the roads because I might be confused for a hunter or because cowboys would think I was out to steal one of their calves. He gave me a head nod as if to swipe a hard line under what he'd just said.

I took his advice, but walking these north-to-south and east-to-west roads was adding about a third more mileage to my trip because my true path was straight southeast. After half an hour, I thought, *What the hell, no one's going to see me out here*, and started walking southeast again, always with a compass in hand, checking it once every minute to make sure I was on the right path. With my trekking poles, I figured I looked more like a bearded praying mantis than a cow thief and that no cowboy in his right mind would confuse me for one of his own.

I reached a gravel road and, low on water, I stopped at a local ranch. I yelled hello and a young man came out of a barn carrying a giant pistol in a holster strapped around his waist. The pistol was ridiculously long—compensatingly long—so long the barrel poked through a hole and dangled nakedly around his lower thigh.

"Sorry about the gun," he said. "Out here, you never know when you're going to need it."

I knew that the Lakota hadn't embarked on any raids in more than a hundred years and figured that there was little crime in these parts, so it was clear that he'd armed himself just for me. I asked him if I could have some water. He said no but proceeded to grab my bottles and fill them up. I could tell I was making him nervous, so I tried to put him at ease by telling him about my trip and remarking how beautiful his land was. I asked him where I might set up my tent, hoping he'd offer his land, but he pointed down the road and told me I could set my tent up wherever I wanted to in that direction.

I found a place down the road to set up my tent, and all through the night, I listened to snowflakes fall onto my thin tent roof, scraping down the sides. *Here it is,* I thought. *Here's winter.*

George Orwell's dilemma in *Down and Out in Paris and London* came to mind. Orwell was living as a poor dishwasher in Paris and was chronically worried about the day he'd finally go broke. But on the day he went broke, he discovered he no longer had anything to worry about. Now he just had something to deal with. I guess I felt the same. Now that winter was here, I could stop waiting for it and just start dealing with it.

The next time I had an Internet connection, I e-mailed Josh to ask him to dip into the kitty of emergency cash I had left him and mail me a winter hat, gloves, an extra pair of socks, a face mask, gaiters, and a four-season tent.

"This is the sheriff. Good morning."

It was eight a.m. and I was camped, as the young man had suggested, along the road in a distant field. On the edges of my tent, snow had piled up in small mounds. The grass glistened everywhere, coated in frost.

I unzipped my tent and began slipping my feet into my frozen boots as I wished the sheriff a good morning, and said, "Well, this probably looks pretty strange, doesn't it?" The sheriff had driven his vehicle over the grass and parked on one side of my tent. When I stepped out of the tent, I saw that strategically positioned in a sort of triangle around me were the sheriff, a middle-aged man wearing a flannel hat with ear flaps, and his son, the young man I'd spoken with the evening before. I looked at the young man and wanted to say, *Dude, what the hell? I thought we were cool?* Instead, I wished him a good morning and thanked him for the water from the night before.

I explained what I was doing, acknowledged how crazy it sounded, mentioned my family, and said I wanted to go on an adventure before I had "to go back to work." Truth was, I never wanted a real job again, but any mention of "family" or "work," I'd learned, instantly made me seem more normal.

"I got a call from the neighbor," said the sheriff. "I just wanted to come out here and make sure you weren't crazy."

"Well, you gotta be a little bit crazy to do something like this," I said, waving my hand at my tent and backpack, playing the only card I had, which was an open display of submissive "please don't shoot me" self-deprecation. I brought the discussion back to the weather, the beauty of the land, and where I was heading today, figuring it would be wise to take control of the direction of the conversation before they could.

The sheriff laughed, but the middle-aged man appeared to be unaffected by my charms.

"You wanna be careful around here," he warned gruffly.

"Does this area have a reputation for crime?" I asked.

"No," he said, taken aback. "But people around here ain't used to what you're doin'. The owner of the land here, if he saw you walkin', he'd a shot ya.

"What you're doin' ain't normal," he continued. "In my lifetime, I've never seen a hiker down this road. And my dad's never seen one in his.

"What you're doin', it's . . . it's . . . strange."

At the moment, I was innocently standing next to my tent, yet he spoke as if I were oiling myself up for a satanic ritual.

"It's strange," he muttered again.

"I'm sorry I raised the alarm," I said. "I'll pack up and be on my way now."

My tone was compassionate and apologetic, but I was flustered. This was the first time in forty days that someone had asked for my ID (not including border crossings). It was suggested that I might get shot. It's a shame, I thought, how I'd just walked through incredible scenery—a stunning stony-cliffed landscape—but no one except for me, a few cows, and a handful of xenophobes would ever get to see it.

In time, though, I'd feel sympathy for them. If I had been in their situation—having lived all their days in remote lands and having had no exposure to hikers, hitchhikers, and bearded travelers—I'd probably feel just as scared and act the same way, too.

"I'd stay on the roads," the gruff man said, which I did for about ten minutes.

10.

The Farmer

BUFFALO, SOUTH DAKOTA—1,274 MILES TO GO

November 12, 2012

←→

"Shysters," Lewis said. "They're damn secretive."

Lewis and Patty are farmers ten miles north of Fallon, Montana. The farmland they lease is directly in the path of the proposed Keystone XL Pipeline. Lewis and Patty weren't at all happy with TransCanada—the company that will build the pipeline—whose land agents, for years, had been approaching homes in the area trying to get landowners to sign contracts.

"Who is responsible if that thing blows up? No one could answer that," Lewis said. "Most of the people want to be treated fairly. This secretive bullshit sits in your craw. How do we know how much money people are getting up in Canada or down in Texas? Land agents won't tell you anything. They keep you isolated. It's all up to you to negotiate."

The landowners were especially irked because TransCanada wanted to use a thinner, cheaper pipe under their land because most of the plains are considered a "low-consequence area." TransCanada was offering only fifteen cents a foot to landowners, but a group of local farmers insisted on thirty dollars. It's difficult to negotiate a fair sum, Lewis said, because all landowners must sign nondisclosures and keep their agreements confidential.

Lewis and Patty's reluctance to embrace the pipeline seemed sensible to me—a position I assumed their private-property-respecting neighbors would theoretically sympathize with. But everyone in the area I talked with seemed either in favor of the pipeline or indifferent to it. I was told things like "Well, the world runs on oil" or "Wouldn't you rather get our oil from our friends up north rather than the terrorists over there?"

After cookies and coffee at Lewis and Patty's, I walked south and crossed the Yellowstone River over the I-94 bridge next to Fallon, Montana.

At the town bar and restaurant, the only place in town where I could get a Wi-Fi signal, a middle-aged lady in a work shirt and loose-fitting Carhartts sat down at my table in front of me. I'd seen her ten miles north of Fallon in her white pickup.

"So what are you doing this for?" she asked. I explained that I was in the mood for a long walk and that I wanted to see the path of the Keystone XL before it was developed.

"What, do you think ethanol is any better?" she exclaimed. Her tone was bitter and accusatory.

"I don't really know . . . " I said, gathering my thoughts, only to be cut off again.

"Look, you're using energy to power that computer," she said, pointing to the socket that my iPad was plugged into. "You don't think we need oil?"

At this point, I had said nothing good or bad about the XL, so I was more than taken aback by her brusqueness. (Plains women, by the way—and I'm speaking generally here—are the brusquest, and therefore the scariest, demographic of women I've ever come across.)

"Well, the planet's warming," I muttered. "We gotta do something."

Despite the bucolic character of the land, which was always a treat for the eye—even the meticulous symmetry of a well-planted hay field—I recognized that these hay fields, and these thousands and thousands of cows, and this livelihood for so many would not exist without large quantities of fossil fuel. Of the top eleven states that consume the most energy per person, seven of those states are on the Great Plains. To exist out here today, vast quantities of oil are necessary.

Not only that, but the cows themselves produce deadly greenhouse gases. Currently, there are 1.4 billion cows on Earth whose farts make up the world's largest source of methane, a greenhouse gas 105 times more potent than carbon dioxide. A 2006 United Nations Food and Agriculture Organization report found that cows generate 18 percent of the world's greenhouse gases—more than worldwide transportation does. In terms of methane, the gassiest states, unsurprisingly, are Great Plains states: Texas, Oklahoma, and Kansas, all of which have sizable oil, natural gas, and cattle industries.

To me, the larger problem wasn't so much a land-use problem, but a cultural, philosophical, and religious problem. Would we do the terrible things to the environment today if we loved the earth more? Would we be where we are if our culture taught us to think of ourselves as part of the world and not just as its lordly stewards?

Many naturalists and environmental writers have their own ethic that they wish everyone would adopt. Aldo Leopold's land ethic amounts to the belief that "A thing is right when it tends to preserve the integrity, stability and beauty of the biotic community. It is wrong when it tends otherwise." Leopold argued that getting a culture to buy into a new ethic isn't impossible, pointing to our now near-universal moral indignation over slavery as evidence that ethics are capable of evolving in dramatic ways.

Leopold believed that it's possible to extend our respect and sense of unity to not just other races and classes, but also to the natural world. This doesn't seem impossible when we acknowledge that cultures in the past—those with pagan and animistic belief systems—thought of the world as a biotic system to which everything and everyone is connected.

Sociobiologist E. O. Wilson believes that the capacity for loving nature, which he calls "biophilia," is already within us. He reminds us that we are drawn to other animals, "thrilled by the prospect of unknown creatures," "riveted by the idea of life on other planets," and that we spend more time in zoos than at professional sports events.

Stephen Jay Gould calls for an emotional bond with nature, and Barry Lopez, a "respectful regard." Dan Flores wonders if we should think of animals like siblings, the way the Plains Indians thought of grizzly bears. Leopold believed that "All ethics rest upon a single premise: that the individual is a member of a community of interdependent parts." E. O. Wilson, who's written extensively on the concept of a conservation ethic, says ethics change when "people look beyond themselves to others, and then to the rest of life." Wilson takes it a step further: We can't just welcome nature under our umbrella; we have to think about life that has yet to exist: "[O]ur perception of time must extend from [our] own life spans to multiple generations and finally to the extended future history of humankind . . . Any ethic worthy of the name has to encompass the distant future."

Wilson believes that we can't expect people in the present to live solely for people in the remote future. He says that we can "never ask people to do anything they consider contrary to their own best interests" and that the "only way to make a conservation ethic work is to ground it in ultimately selfish reasoning." A new ethic will be adopted only if it presents a "material gain for themselves, their kin, and their tribe," perhaps in the form of "a healthful environment, the warmth of kinship, right-sounding moral structures, sure-bet economic gain, and a stirring of nostalgia and sentiment."

This relationship with nature does not come automatically. Wilson argues that the "relationships of ecology and the human mind are too intricate to be understood entirely by unaided intuition" and "common sense." Wilson's saying that we are not predisposed to feel empathy for the ozone or sacrifice for generations that have yet to be born or embrace grizzly bears as brothers. Education is the only way to instill this ethic: "Only through an unusual amount of education and reflective thought do people come to respond emotionally to far-off events and hence place a high premium on posterity." Wilson, who studied ants as a boy, believes it's more than possible to come to love another life form if gifted with knowledge of it. But loving future generations is something else entirely. For Wilson, looking out for the earth for the sake of our descendants has less to do with acting on their behalf and more to do with creating wholesome, conscientious, and contented lives for ourselves. In other words, to care for the future is to live well in the present. "What do we really owe our remote descendants?" Wilson asks. "Nothing . . . But what do we owe ourselves in planning for them? Everything."

In the end, I didn't think a new ethic, in and of itself, would be enough to solve our environmental problems. More of us might come to see our relationship with the planet in a new light, but there'd always be threats from the powerful, the ambitious, and the money hungry. Even the Native Americans, with their strong conservation ethics, participated in the nineteenth-century slaughter of the buffalo and beaver, helping to bring each to the brink of extinction. A new ethic, at best, would merely make possible the government initiatives that currently lack public support.

Still, I wanted to believe a conservation ethic could exist. But when speaking to the woman in Fallon, and a lot of the folks I met along the way, I guessed that I'd probably never see one take hold in my lifetime. She drives long distances to and from her pasture every day. She might run a tractor over hundreds of acres of hay fields. Scaling down, smaller farms, higher taxes on diesel: These sorts of changes the experts recommend would be appalling, unthinkable—offensive, even—to someone like her. It's no wonder why well-meaning scientists are so quickly dismissed, and why global warming is denied by those whose livelihoods are so reliant on fossil fuels.

"I'd hate to see you get shot," said a local, who kindly handed over an orange hunting vest as I cooked my dinner under Fallon's park pavilion.

I continued on toward Baker, Montana, now in a bright orange vest. I walked through miles and miles of canyons. When I'd approach the edge of a canyon wall, I would worry that I wouldn't be able to find a way down. But at every canyon rim, I was quick to find a path blazed by cows that safely led down and up the steep rock-and-dirt walls.

The town of Baker sat beneath a gray overcast sky. When I first caught sight of the town, I was standing next to an abandoned windmill that had only half its blades and creaked hauntingly with each passing gust.

North of town were dozens of pump jacks, some white, bearing streaks of rust; others, pitch-black. Some were slowly dunking their proboscises into the ground, but most stood frozen, paralyzed, dead, having long ago sucked dry the pools of black nectar that once gave them life.

In town, behind hillocks of scrap heap, I could see the top of a crane busy moving metal. The town, like a lot of small towns on the plains, had an air of decrepitude, but when I entered, I was shocked to see the bustle of business: hundreds of new pickups were parked in front of bars and motels; Hummers growled down Main Street; trailers were everywhere, housing all the temporary workers who were building two pipelines in the area.

Baker was booming, but the pipeliners would eventually leave, the motels would empty, the bars would cut back on servers, and things would resume as they had. The money that once came in in such abundance would, in time, be squandered and forgotten.

I walked into the post office, where I picked up several packages. Josh had sent me four days' worth of food, a brand-new four-season tent, and winter gear: a merino wool shirt, a pair of gaiters (for walking through snow), a new pair of gloves, a new hat, a pair of hiking boots, two pairs of wool socks, and two new pairs of underwear. I mailed him my old tent and comfortably bedded down in my new and much warmer shelter.

. . .

"For someone with a college education, what you're doing is pretty stupid," said Abigail, who ran the town newspaper for Buffalo, South Dakota. "I mean, it's really stupid."

I was in Buffalo, sitting at Abigail's kitchen table. She and her family offered to give me a room in their home for the night.

Abigail was, and had been, laying on the criticism pretty thick, but I was dumbly content, scarfing down the eighth pancake she'd made me, which was slathered in butter and dripping with blueberry syrup. We'd had this discussion, it seemed, a half-dozen times already, and I'd long ago given up trying to justify my trip or parry her attacks with fresh retorts. "These pancakes are excellent," I said.

Year after year, Abigail and her husband hosted foreign-exchange students, and now they were caring for two Norwegian high school teenagers, who were going to play in the state championship football game the next day, which was the talk of the town, as was the election.

It was election night and President Obama would be announced the victor early in the evening. Four years ago, I was deeply moved when Obama won. Everyone was crying. Jesse Jackson was crying. Oprah was crying. I may have had some weird allergic reaction thing going on in my eye. But rather than ushering in a golden age of democracy and renewing hope in American politics, the Obama election— whether because of a misrepresentation in character, a lack of will, or simply complicated political limitations—made the young Americans who helped get him into office lose hope in government, in our democracy, and in him. Watching the results on TV, I felt none of the glory of four years ago—only a mild relief that we at least had made the best of a bad situation.

Once a source of hope, politics to me then was no more than a semiyearly obligation, like traveling home to attend a distant friend's wedding. I watched Obama give his acceptance speech with the same sense of wry commiseration I felt when watching that friend inflict himself with the cruel and unusual punishment of life-long monogamy: It was a celebration where I wasn't sure what I was celebrating. I turned off the TV, changed into my thermals, and went to bed.

I felt as if I were in a giant orange balloon being tossed in a stormy sky. But I was only in South Dakota, on the ground, in my orange tent next to a murky lake.

There was a storm outside that the Weather Channel called Brutus. My tent fluttered violently, pounded by twenty-five-mile-per-hour winds. Freezing rain pitter-pattered against my tent walls all day long. The cold, a manageable thirty degrees Fahrenheit, dropped down to eight, and all sides of my tent were shaking with the wind except the one nearest my head, which was solid, frozen inside by my exhalations and outside by the freezing rain. I pushed against it every now and then, and with enough force, I'd hear a loud crack and the ice outside would crash to the ground.

Despite the storm, I was cozy in my tent, maybe more so because I was stuck in it. I thought mostly hopeful, happy thoughts. I looked forward to the days and years to come. I ate as much in the tent as I did when I was on the move and eagerly read the third installment of Edmund Morris's Teddy Roosevelt biography, *Colonel Roosevelt*. Normally, I'd resent being stuck like this, but I'd just walked fifteen days straight, doing between fifteen and twenty-five miles a day, and I saw the need for a good long rest.

I woke up on the second day without any expectation of hiking. The forecast—which I was able to check on my iPad (whose battery was beginning to run alarmingly low)—said the weather was going to get worse: colder, snowier, and windier. I put on all of my clothes: thermal underwear, two pairs of socks, five layers of shirts, plus my rain suit, a beanie, a faux-fur hat, and a pair of gloves. I went outside to fill up my water bottles from the lake, which was only partly frozen over, and to hammer in my tent stakes as deep into the frozen ground as they'd go.

I rationed my iPad usage so I could read throughout the day and night, took a three-hour nap, and consumed an inexcusable amount of food. The freezing rain stopped momentarily, right before sunset, so I went out to use the bathroom and climbed a hill to see if I could spot a road, a house, or some sanctum of safety, if just for precautionary reasons. But I couldn't see anything except a herd of curious deer, who had caught sight of me by the lake. The sky, though, on its western end, looked as if it were on fire: a brilliant orange wrapped in a heavy quilt of big dark-blue clouds.

Staring at this orange sky—whose color probably portended a more vicious stage of the storm—I was dazzled. It had nothing to do with being at the mercy of weather extremes or pushing my limits. Rather, I felt the presence of something spectacular—sinister, perhaps, but no less spectacular—and it occurred to me that there are great truths bound by beauty, truths I could not comprehend, but truths that were there, pregnant with mysterious meaning.

Worried that the clouds would bring a fog or blizzard that might impair my visibility—perhaps so much that I wouldn't be able to find my tent—I ran back as quickly as I could. The grass and cacti and thistles were frozen over, plump with ice coating their contours, forming a field of brittle, glistening stalagmites. As I ran, the ground shattered, tinkling like a shaken Christmas tree.

I slept restlessly. The cold was too cold, and my sleeping bag, over the past several nights, had accumulated moisture and was no longer living up to its five-degrees-Fahrenheit promise. My iPad's battery had died, so my digital library was gone, but I'd taken note of the forecast and saw that tomorrow would be as cold and windy but clearer.

In the morning, I packed my things with numb fingers and headed southeast. Less than an hour into my hike, I saw that the forecast was mistaken. The sun, which was bright and blinding moments before, was lost behind the encroaching blimp of dark clouds. Snow began to fall, and I could see only a mile in the distance. I was being overtaken by a blizzard, and I worried that I wouldn't be able to set up my tent in these winds with my frozen fingers. I saw, however, an abandoned barn. As I approached, an enormous great horned owl leaped out from a glassless window, and I felt awful because I'd scared it from its home right before the storm. I picked up scrap wood and started a fire with tattered rope. I made a meal and held my sleeping bag over the fire to dry it out. Hot steam escaped my bag and instantly dissipated into the crisp air.

Out here, in this abandoned barn, I thought about how townspeople all along this hike were always calling me "crazy" or "insane," as Abigail did back in Buffalo. When you're called these things every day, it can have an effect. I'd wonder, *Am I crazy? Maybe I shouldn't be traveling cross-country? Is what I'm doing . . . wrong?*

Such thoughts were like burrs stuck to my pant leg, prickling me every few strides. It wasn't until I got out onto the open prairie or under the frozen fireworks of a starry night or in an unusual place like this abandoned barn that I'd finally be able to shake them off. When the ground is hard, the landscape half-wild, the weather pleasant, and the pain of walking gone, I'd feel a wild joy swell in my chest, a joy known only to the solitary traveler of many miles.

One day, I didn't come across a road. The prairie was mostly flat, the ground gently lifting and falling. As I went on, the land became hilly, then turned into canyons with steep ravines full of dwarf hackberry trees and dried piles of cow manure. There isn't a geographical name for this sort of terrain. It was a magnificent combination of prairie, hill, and canyon. The hills were shaggy and green, though their grass-bald cliffs were colored a pale dirt brown. When I got to the top of one of these cliffs, I looked toward the horizon and saw grander— real mountains—in the distance. There weren't any villages, farmhouses, or industry—nothing but undulating hills. Some were a wild grainy green, and others, the bigger ones, pyramids of loose rock, some of which appeared to be topped with a sculpture or a decorative stone pinnacle, but were, on closer inspection, clusters of boulders that nature had chosen to strangely arrange.

I was constantly awestruck by the unexpected. And sometimes I'd be overcome with this joy, this love, this ecstasy. Whatever it was, it would linger, and sometimes I'd carry it with me for hours. I'd be overcome with a strange love for this rock, this blade of grass, that white cloud tearing into pieces, this body, this life. I wanted to fall to the ground and hug it. I wanted to suck all the air from the sky and eat all the dirt and consume everything so it and I were finally one. I had come to feel this with an astonishing regularity.

Every day there was a new trial. There was someone new to meet, something new to think, something new to learn, something new to see with every step, every turn. It was an infusion of newness! We weren't meant to be dishwashers, doing the same thing day in and day out. No, I knew from this sustained joy, this steady percolation of fulfillment, that we were meant for lives of variety, of novelty, of adventure. Immersed in this constant newness, when every step was exploratory, every interaction novel, and every day completely different from the previous, it was hard to think of ever going back to the dullness of the normal, the expected, the planned. Looking over the great white windy plains, I didn't think I was crazy. Rather, I thought that a life lived not half-wild is a life only half-lived.

11.

The Electrician

November 27, 2012

←→

While my legs and hips and back felt strong, and my feet were no longer plagued with cuts and blisters and gashes, the physical toil of walking every day caused a weariness to settle into my muscles and bones, into the very roots of me, a weariness that I knew wouldn't go away with a day's, a week's, or even a month's rest.

Because of the waning daylight (it was getting dark around four thirty p.m. now) I was limited to walking from six thirty a.m. to three forty-five p.m., making it all the more difficult to reach my twenty-miles-a-day goal. To compensate for the lack of daylight, I pushed myself hard, taking as few breaks as I could, reminding myself—when my feet and shoulders were aching—that I'd have the whole evening for lounging and reading and writing.

In Midland, South Dakota, where I was going to pick up another food package, I spent the evening at a bar, where I ate a double bacon cheeseburger and charged my electronics. The bar also functioned as the town's gas station, grocery store, and casino, the last of which was located in a small dark room behind old-style saloon doors.

I sat quietly in the corner trying to write, but the bar became rowdy and I wasn't able to focus, so I entertained myself with the Broncos-Chargers game on the television. The conversations in the room ranged from branding cows to hammering fence posts to Kim Kardashian to a very sincere debate about what it means to be a good son.

Greg, an electrician, was the first of the bunch to befriend me. He told me that when I went to the bathroom the whole bar wondered aloud who I was and what I was doing. "They thought you were a monster," he said, laughing. What really confused them were my trekking poles.

When the bartender asked me later on what I used my "skiing poles" for, she, clearly unsatisfied with my explanation, gave me a dubious look and seemed even more suspicious. When Greg announced to the crowd what I'd set out to do, the bartender told me I'd get shot if I walked over so-and-so's property, a warning I dismissed because I'd heard warnings like this one in nearly every bar I stopped in. "Oh, he'll shoot you!" she said. I gathered that these weren't so much warnings but rather reaffirming boasts about how rugged their land is and how tough the people who dwell on it are. The men at most all of my stops would warn me about cougars, talking about the big cats with intimate knowledge, as if they had monthly wrestling contests with the animal even though no one had ever even seen one.

"Has he shot anyone before?" I asked the bartender.

"Well, no," she said.

Greg called himself a black sheep because he was one of the very few people who favored progressive politics in South Dakota.

Throughout the night, the bartender screamed at him with equal parts affection and scorn, "Obama lover!" Greg laughed and tried to engage them in a political discussion, but the bartender and the rest of the bar deflected his efforts.

Greg suggested I sleep on his floor for the night.

He ordered two more beers ("two for the ditch") and I followed his truck to his home in the center of town. I sat with him in his trailer at his kitchen table, which was cluttered with a rat's nest of magazines, envelopes, and a pair of Hanes briefs, which he saw no reason to remove.

"What do you think about the legalization of marijuana?" Greg asked, while constructing a makeshift pipe out of a Coca-Cola can, piercing a hole into the polar bear's head.

"I'm okay with it," I said.

He told me that South Dakotans are pro-business, but that they're "South Dakotans at heart" and don't like it when big corporations force them to do anything. Still, he said, they rarely vote in their best interests, unthinkingly favoring the party of the wealthy when it might be better for them to vote for politicians who more honestly represent the middle class.

When I asked him why they do this, he said, "People around here don't know how to have an intellectual conversation." His voice was a slow, slurred baritone, drunken but wise.

I knew what he meant. I'd been walking for two months, but it wasn't until that moment with Greg that I felt completely free to share my thoughts, uncensored, with another person. It is difficult to find a true conversant: one who is not ruled by prejudice or dogma, and whose opinions are alive and vibrant, living documents of the mind, subject to evolution and amendment.

In the morning, when I awoke, I found that Greg had already left for work so I packed my things, wrote him a thank-you note, and picked up my package at the post office. I walked down gravel roads and then hopped a barbed-wire fence into the prairie, where I didn't get shot.

'd been getting most of my water from the windmill springs that cows drink from. But I was now on a stretch of ground where the windmills were all dilapidated, so I had to resort to my time-tested tactic of knocking on the doors of lonely houses.

Spotting one from a bluff, I walked a long dirt road with barbed wire on each side with cows chewing cud and staring at me in a more familiar way than usual, as these were obviously more acquainted with humans than the usual quick-to-scatter cows I'd been dealing with.

At the home ahead were two hunters in camo, holding rifles. They were your typical goateed, portly "big white guys."

Two dead deer were hanging by their hind legs from a wooden scaffold.

"Good afternoon," I called out. "I'm on a long walk across the country. Could I trouble you for some water?"

The younger hunter, in his early forties, was visibly shaken by my presence so, like most scared people, he put on an air of surly toughness.

"This ain't our place," he said. "So we can't help you."

"Oh. No problem. But do you mind telling me where I am?" I said, pulling out my map. "I'm headed toward the town of Winner."

"It's nowhere near here. You're going to have to backtrack about ten miles to get to a road."

Packing up four
and a half month's
worth of food.

My broken little
toe days before
start of hike.

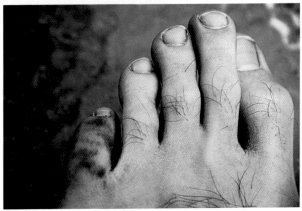

Getting a ride with
a Nation Guard JAG
in Wyoming.

Hitchhiking with
an oil worker in
Montana.

Hitchhiking into
Hardisty, Alberta.

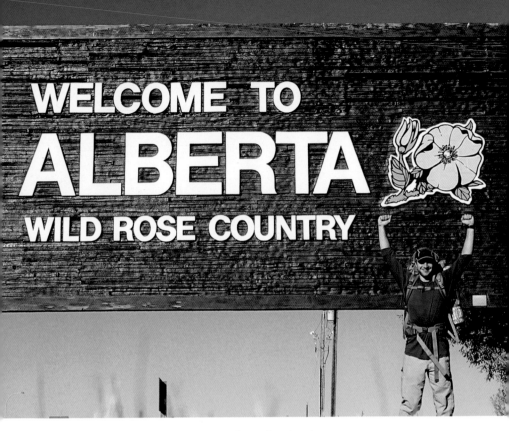

Across the Canadian border.

Folks picking me up in Alberta after football practice.

Boreal forest of
Alberta en route to
the tar sands.

ABOVE: Tailings pond.

RIGHT: Fields of coke.

Hardisty, Alberta, the northern terminus of the proposed Keystone XL pipeline.

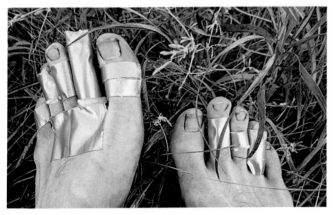

LEFT: Managing blisters with duct tape.

BELOW: Alberta prairie.

Harold with his family in Consort, Alberta.

McNeill, Alberta.

Sandhills in Alberta, Canada.

Saskatchewan, Canada.

Ron Caswell near Bracken, Saskatchewan.

A windbreak on the Montana prairie.

Montana hay field.

South Dakota.

ABOVE:
Black Angus cattle.

LEFT:
Me in South Dakota.

LEFT: A warm welcome in Albion, Nebraska from anti-XL activists. *(Courtesy of Adrian Olivera)*

RIGHT: Rick "The Governor" Hammond and I. *(Courtesy of Meghan Hammond)*

BELOW: Caterpillar bulldozer near McCool Junction, Nebraska.

UPPER LEFT: Harold, me, and Maralee.

UPPER RIGHT: "Kansas" the dog.

BOTTOM: Entering Oklahoma.

Texas cow.

Mike Bishop near Douglass, Texas.

Pipe being laid in Texas.

Storms and I getting caught trespassing.

Approaching the Valero refinery in Port Arthur, Texas.
(Courtesy of Pete Churton)

The last step of the journey in the Sabine Netches Waterway.
(Courtesy of Woody Welch)

"That's good to know," I said. "But I've been walking cross-country. And it would be unthinkable for me to backtrack so many miles. I've walked close to twenty miles. I'm about done for the day."

"Well, you can't cross this property. You're going to have to walk back and find a road. You'll have to take it north, then east, then you can cross the river there."

"Well, if I have to, I'll go that way," I said, knowing there was no way I'd go that way. "Would you mind at least showing me where I am on the map?"

He pulled out his hunting knife and placed the sharp edge on the map, just inches from my hand.

The owner of the place—which was evidently a hunting camp—came out with his little girl and a big smile, took an interest in my hike, hooked me up with some water, which, I was glad to see, shamed the hunter for his inhospitality, and gave me permission to walk his land and cross the White River.

Is there anything more rhythmic than the motion of walking? There is an undeniable elegance in its swinging limbs, its clockwork symmetry, its mechanical momentum, its choreography of balance. The human stride is one of our biological blessings—a dazzlingly complicated operation that requires little conscious thought. It frees our minds to plan and dream and think as our body lurches forward, handling the business of breaths, pulses, pores, and the million rotating gears necessary for just one successful step of an amble. Your shoulders and hips rotate. Your arms gently wag, greased by pints of sweat flooding from your armpits. Your back is straight. Your head is level, looking ahead, lightly bobbing with each footfall. Your knee bends, and your leg straightens, bends and straightens, bends and straightens. Your body falls forward but is saved by the next placement of your foot that meets the ground in front of you at just the right second. The ball of your heel is planted, the arch of your foot rolls with the shape of the terrain, and your toes launch you forward into the majesty of bipedal locomotion: an evolutionary triumph that has freed our hands to build and throw and gather, granting us the means to leave our past in the confines of the jungle and set our sights on the unconquered glories of the open savannah.

There may be nothing more human than the act of putting one foot in front of the other. It's a potentially unwieldy method of transportation when you think about it. Most other animals have another two legs on the ground (or, in the case of primates, long arms) to keep them balanced and upright. We are the awkward unicyclists of the animal kingdom. (Remember that we spend most of the time walking with only one limb securing us to the ground.) Each step forward is like a leap of faith—an act of hope that we won't topple and will land okay so long as we take another step and another step after that. And perhaps there's no better symbol for the boldness of the great human experiment than the walk, as each springy step contains the same extravagance, cocksureness, and audacity present in the greatness of our pyramids and the arrogance of our tar-sand pits.

You're in that late-morning, mid-afternoon sweet spot when the soreness of yesterday has dissipated and the soreness of today has yet to surface. You begin to feel a dull and pleasant heaviness overtake your leg and butt muscles. You feel your thighs turning into rock-hard muscle, your stomach flattening, your calves turning into two speed bags of death. The calories boil away, and you feel as if you were the most in-shape person on Earth: a healthy, hot, hiking sex god. Time slows down. Days get longer. You feel as if you've walked an hour, and you look down at your watch to see that only ten minutes have passed.

Going on a long walk across the country is such a change of lifestyle that it's about as close as you can get to experiencing life as a different person. A journey is so full of unfamiliar circumstances that you have no choice but to deal with life's trials in unfamiliar ways. To deal with the mental, physical, and emotional rigors of a journey—when every day, every step, every person is different from the previous one—you have to take on a multitude of new roles because your old ordinary self is just not equipped to handle this cascade of newness.

Normally, in North Carolina, I played the role of a gardening, writing, van-dwelling recluse. In Alaska, I was the solitary, nature-loving book nut. Back at my parents' home in New York, I was a beer-drinking, video game–playing bedroom hermit. Each place brought out a slightly different side of me, but wherever I went, I was essentially the same crowd-shy introvert who favored being by himself. It was as if gravity—or some indomitable force—would pull me back to that persona no matter where I lived, despite the fact that I didn't always want to return to that rather limited person. Yet I'd feel a dull comfort in my own company and in my routine of eating, jogging, reading, writing, working, and movie watching. The routine of my life followed me everywhere.

But when you travel—especially when you travel alone—you have to adapt to a whole new routine because that old solitary, sedentary person you were just won't cut it. You *have* to change. You *have* to broaden. You *have* to become not just another type of person but many different types of people. Of course, part of me would remain my normal introverted self, but I'd also have to become sociable, extroverted, charming, cunning, crafty, bullshitting, bold, confident, and careful.

If you've ever traveled for a period of time with a group, you've probably noticed that the individuals within the group will almost instantly specialize and adopt well-defined roles. I once went on a two-month-long canoe voyage with two other guys, and within days, without anyone verbally assigning roles, we automatically adopted routines and roles. One guy became the leader, navigator, and canoe repairer. Another became the emissary who did all of our talking for us. I became the expedition's baker, pot washer, and mule. It was an efficient setup, and we were more effective as a team this way, and our daily tasks suited each of our ordinary personalities. But I regret that for those whole two months I never once looked at a map. I never learned to navigate, repair a canoe, or suavely persuade a property owner to let us camp on his land.

When you travel alone, you have no choice but to play *all* of the roles. You have to be the whole team. You have to be all seven samurai. On my hike, I was the navigator, cook, mule, diplomat, tent erector, water purifier, blogger, book reader, psychologist, emotional picker-upper, singer, conversant, dog whisperer, bodyguard, nutrition-ist, hemmer of tears, cleaner of self, camp organizer, logistics coordi-nator, medic, and wannabe environmental crusader.

And in so doing, I felt like a richer, more self-reliant person. All of my senses had become keener. I was constantly looking to horizons, seeking good paths. When stealth was required, I listened carefully for cows or trucks. Going over a hill, for the first time in my life, I smelled an animal (a faintly pleasant oily wildness) before I heard or saw it: a coyote, half-amazed, half-terrified, tripping over itself as it sprinted away, too bewildered to take its eyes off of me. My mind and body, awakened from their torpor, felt invigorated, healthy, alive.

I'd always been extremely self-conscious—wondering what other people thought of me—and this somewhat nagging tendency was now reprogrammed so I could figure out what was going on in other people's heads. And, naturally, most people were initially leery of me. I did everything I could to put them at ease. I was aware of and controlled my every facial expression and hand gesture. I knew to never dig into my pockets without casually alluding to what I was about to retrieve. "Can you show me where I am on my map?" I'd say, before putting my hand into my back pocket. I'd look at people in their eyes and keep a healthy distance between me and them until I sensed that I'd earned their trust. I'd compliment the beauty of their land, make some remark about the weather, my family, my work, and make fun of myself for undertaking a journey in winter. I'd use "sir" and "ma'am" and say "good afternoon" instead of "hey." I'd go from being melancholic and solitary one moment to affable and extroverted the next, and I'd wear one mask as genuinely as the other.

It's a cliché and misleading to say that we're "transformed" by our journeys. No one is ever really transformed into another human being. At the end of the journey, you're more or less the same bundle of cells, memories, and values that you were beforehand. What changes, though, is that you're able to make others believe that you're this confident, capable, charming person (or some other set of uncharacteristic qualities). At first, you feel as if you were deceiving others and yourself and that this person whom you're pretending to be is just a game you're playing or a strategy you're using. But after wearing the million masks a journey requires you to wear, it's no longer so easy by the end to distinguish yourself from the selves you've been faking. They merge, you expand, and when you do pull off an impressive and uncharacteristic exhibition of charm (or some other uncharacteristic feat), you're left wondering, *Did I just do that? Was that fake or was that . . . me?*

To go on a walk is to think. We might as well call it "to go on a think" because there's nothing to do but think. (It was no surprise to learn from author Robert Macfarlane that the Tlicho Indians of northwestern Canada use the same word to describe "footprint" and "knowledge.") No, you are a moving monastery, a university of one, walking the contours of your mind the same way your feet travel over the hills and fields in front of you.

Where does the mind go during a period of near-endless solitude on a long walk?

Walking across the plains is sort of like walking in a dream. Once you've entered into a state of peace and quiet—when you can no longer hear the hum of traffic, the chatter of voices, and the constant presence of civilization—the subconscious comes to the surface and shows itself to you.

You have wakeful dreams. Projected onto your mind's screen is a slideshow of your past and reels of old memories. Your subconscious has you cornered, whipping open its raincoat, unveiling to you your fears, regrets, embarrassments, and fantasies that you'd ordinarily catch glimpses of only in your sleep. You see what's been making the floorboards creak up in the attic of your mind. You find out what bodies need to be raked up from the murky swamps of your inner self. It takes you to unexpected places.

A long serene walk on a serene landscape doesn't always produce serene thoughts. I thought of the time in the fourth grade when I accidentally and loudly kicked over a tin garbage pail and was laughed at by the class, and I swear I felt the same intensity of embarrassment at twenty-nine on the prairie that I did at nine in the classroom. I remembered, as an eleven-year-old paperboy, when I was chased by a bully wielding a garter snake. I twisted my Huffy bike around, pedaled as fast as I could, and just barely escaped, subsequently and shamefully bursting into tears in front of my father when I told him that I had more papers to deliver but couldn't do it by myself. I thought of my failed first kiss when, at sixteen, at the end of an afternoon date, I kissed my girlfriend of two months (it took me a while, I know!), hastily exited her car, mounted the stairs in my parents' home, victoriously raised my arms for finally doing it, and then dropped them in abject misery after I replayed the scene in my head and realized that I'd just pecked her right nostril. I'd think of the time when, as an eighteen-year-old landscaper on a college campus, I drove a golf cart around campus to pick up trash. Once, when I left the golf cart to pick a piece of plastic off the ground, the golf cart rolled down a hill and crashed into a plumber's truck, putting a giant dent into his passenger-side door. When I realized that no one had seen what had happened, I got in the cart, took off, and never told anyone about it.

I thought of all the arguments I wanted to have but never did. I played out all these melees in my head, defeating my opponent with astonishing rationale and eloquence. It didn't matter how many years had passed; everyone's insult to me still stung just as badly. Every embarrassment was just as devastating. I thought of the hunter's meanness for days, and my hatred for him lingered like a throbbing infection. And I wished that playing out these memories would purge the worst of them from my brain—finally kicking them out—but they still come back today in pretty much the same form.

I'd think of my old dog, Buster, a golden retriever from my boy-hood that I adored, and I'd think about how I'd used to believe that he and my father—his main disciplinarian—had an icy relationship and how that belief changed when I saw how Buster would greet my father in the laundry room after he came home from the night shift: an un-characteristic and dignified leap up to my dad's belly, where he rested his two front paws and received an affectionate head rub. I'd think about the time we all put Buster's cancer-filled body to sleep in the fall of my first year of college and how my mother, father, and I rubbed him and cooed over him and cried as the vet injected the deadly flu-ids while my brother, ashamed of his grief, stood facing the corner of the room. I thought about how I felt that in the death of our beloved dog our family, in our shared grief, was the closest it had ever been and ever will be. I'd think of my dad, my sweet, old, kind dad, and think about how he won't always be here, and I'd mutter, in tears, "My papa!"

I'd think of women. You'd think that on a solo journey where I went days without seeing people—especially women of a courtable age—that my sexuality would dim and that I'd fall into a state of de-sireless serenity. I'd be a celibate, an ambulatory monk, a levelheaded eunuch whose stride had quickened now that his legs were liberated from having to awkwardly rub and bump against his sweaty jumble of anatomy. Perhaps this would have been the case if I had been living in one of these sleepy prairie ghost towns, where the prospect of being the object of a woman's desire was next to nil. Perhaps then I would have experienced some reduction in testosterone, some curbing of passions, some new appreciation for sitting around the town's lonely diner for a game of gin with a group of men. But the act of travel seems to enliven sensations that frankly have no use in a land as barren of women as the northern prairie. But here's the thing: Because I didn't know what lay ahead, the presence of even the remotest possibility of romance was enough to make me stupidly hopeful and constantly eager to venture onward and see what was to come. Perhaps at the next house I approached to ask for water, there would be a sweet-faced Hutterite girl, whose culturally prescribed policy of chastity would, in our moment of passion, be thrown to the wind along with her kerchief head scarf. Or maybe I'd find some bronze-skinned native prairie goddess foraging for camas bulbs. Or maybe a Czech milkmaid. My Antonia!

When I walked, I found myself revisiting all of my sexual encounters of the past, all bookmarked in my memory for easy retrieval: the night of sweaty tent sex; the ground-shaking first times; the purrs of pleasure; the flings; the ferocious honeymoon reunions; the soft, sweet loving embraces. My chest would tighten slightly, my loins would tingle, and my testicles felt as if someone had flipped a switch, turning on a burning light in my underwear that might be sending blinding sunbeams through the holes of my barbed-wire-torn pants. I'd become erect and I'd shove my walking sticks under one arm and throttle my hardness like a gear shift, holding it in midstride, half out of frustration and half to give myself an extra tingle of pleasure. I'd become jittery about my next encounter, another woman of her own particular shape, smell, laugh, and smile. Perhaps she'd be in the next farmhouse. The next town.

Here's the thing about travel. Even if nothing ends up happening, and even if your longings go unanswered, there's always the *potential* for something to happen, and therefore there is the *excitement* that something might happen. And even if you don't get satisfaction, some part of you remains in a near-constant state of excitement. And if there's a better feeling to have consistently in life than excitement, I don't know it. More than anything, potential pitches the traveler forward. Fate, on a journey, is no longer an abstract concept; it's who you're going to meet and what you're going to see tomorrow.

I walked the prairie for a good ways with a rock-hard and usually pretty uncomfortable boner, which pointed straight southeast. My life was in front of me, not behind, and my springy fifth limb was apparently eager to see what lay ahead, extending itself yearningly a few humble inches in advance of the rest of me. And even though, as the weeks passed, I realized more and more that my fantasies would go unfulfilled, it didn't stop me from fantasizing or from enjoying the fantasizing. Honestly, the act of desiring was just as enlivening, and maybe even as satisfying, as actually attaining the object of my desires. Life becomes an adventure when there's always another adventure on the path ahead.

I crossed the White River in southern South Dakota, holding my trekking poles in one hand and my hiking boots in the other. While my feet had toughened, they were more sensitive than ever to cold water for some reason. It felt as if each foot were a rod into which the shallow river channeled its freezing charge. I screamed and cursed as loudly as I could the whole way across.

I cleaned my feet, which were coated in sand with a thatch of grass. I put on my boots and climbed a steep embankment, where I reentered the prairie.

The prairie was as desolate as ever. I couldn't see any homes, and I crossed a rarely traveled gravel road every few miles. I hopped a barbed-wire fence into a cow pasture and casually walked up to a herd of Black Angus cows.

These cows, I observed, weren't running away from me as they normally would. I yelled, "Get outta here, cows!" and waved my poles in the air, trying to freak them out, but they moved only a few yards to the left and right, creating a narrow corridor, which I had no choice but to walk through.

The land was flat except for a gentle downward slope that led to a creek that had dried up. I walked down the slope, and in the grassy creek bed there were another dozen cows staring at me. The cows that I had just passed had gathered and were following me down the hill. I had moving cows behind me and motionless cows in front of me. My heart thumped. My pulse raced. I became unseasonably sweaty. I'd just taken a hit of adrenaline. All the pains and sores that I had been walking with were completely forgotten, and I now had one and only one aim: get away from these cows!

I was surrounded. And then I heard it. It was a rolling thunder, a gurgle from the skies—the sort that would bring a family out to the front porch to watch a summer thunderstorm. I took off at a jog.

I looked back for a moment, one blip of a second, and caught a glimpse of the most terrifying, amazing, makes-my-legs-wobbly thing I'd ever set my eyes on. It was a tidal wave of black muscle pouring down the hill, a horde of Black Angus cows just ten yards behind me, their hooves launching tufts of grass into the air, their huge bodies moving across the treeless prairie in a thunderous, ground-shaking roar.

The worst of my fears had come true.

I was being attacked by cows.

There was only one word on my mind, which communicated itself to me in a not-so-hushed tone of not-so-poised determination.

Run.

12.

The Denier

MILLS, NEBRASKA—995 MILES TO GO

December 3, 2012

← →

The cows in front of me scattered, and I sprinted down the slope along the creek bed as fast as I could under the heft of my pack. I flung my trekking poles off to the side. I needed to get my pack off so I could run. Really run.

I unbuckled the waist buckle of my pack. The ground trembled beneath the cows' hooves. I lifted my hands to my chest to unbuckle the top buckle of my backpack. The weight of the pack had shifted, and the belt was straining in both directions, making it impossible to unclasp the buckle with the normal push of a button.

"C'mon!" I growled through clenched teeth, struggling to unbuckle it, still running. The cows were getting closer.

"C'MON!"

It unbuckled. The pack fell off of my back like a rocket booster. I didn't have a moment to appreciate that I'd just dropped two-thousand-dollars' worth of gear to be trampled by the pursuing herd.

My arms pumped furiously, the tips of my hiking boots dug into the soft grass, my leg muscles plunged me forward in great groin-stretching leaps. In midstride—and I don't know why I did this—I flung off my orange hunting vest.

I ran along the dry creek and began to mount the slope in front of me. I had no idea how many cows were behind me. Twenty? Fifty? (I submit this as a new proverb: "When you're not sure how many cows are chasing you, don't stop to count.") I ran up the slope and saw another barbed-wire fence ahead.

My face was bright red, my eyes squinted, my arms pumping, hands karate chopping, forehead veins bulging, digestive system impressively still functioning.

I made for the fence, throwing myself onto the ground, and rolled safely beneath the bottom wire. I lay there gasping for air, staring up into the dusky gray overcast sky. The cows came to a halt at the fence, and I stood up and looked into the eyes of my enemies, feeling a mix of relief from my escape and dread as I realized my fear of cows was back and that I'd have to carry it with me for the rest of my hike.

It was about an hour before sunset. I knew I needed to get my pack, which, of course, had my tent, clothes, and sleeping bag. I ducked under the fence and walked toward the herd screaming like a maniac. The cows stepped back a few yards but then started walking toward me again, so I walked back to the fence and decided that I need to change my strategy.

I walked the perimeter of the fence, seeking a cow-free route to get my stuff. I told myself, *Just do it*, ducked under the fence, and scurried to the creek. I worried that I wouldn't be able to find the pack, but there it was, untrampled, sitting on its side. A black cow with a white face climbed down the hill and trotted behind me, so I ran along the creek shouldering my pack, forgetting about the search for my dear trekking poles. The creek bed was all muck, so my feet and ankles got sucked into the earth, but I pushed forward, escaping the white-faced Skeletor cow, set my pack outside the fence, and commenced another mission to find my poles, which I did find, though my orange hunting vest was never retrieved.

The prairie gave way to canyons, and I set up my tent at the bottom of one next to another dry creek bed. As I lay in my sleeping bag staring at my tent ceiling, I heard the march of hooves nearby and then a deep moan. I unzipped my tent door. A thin gauze of clouds sat in front of a crescent moon, bright and fuzzy. I vaguely spotted the bodies of black cows walking next to the creek, black ghouls floating across the grass. I tied my bootlaces and uncapped my bear spray in case more split-second heroics were called for. In the morning, I reached another barbed-wire fence and entered yet another cow pasture and did the only thing I could: I screamed and waved my poles over my head, advancing headlong toward the herd.

I was eating a pumpkin pie with a plastic spoon while hiking down Highway 18 in southern South Dakota. A homeowner, who'd seen me walk past his home, thought I might be hungry so he had jumped in his truck and brought me three-fourths of his leftover Thanksgiving dessert. This was one of several kindnesses offered to me near the town of Winner, South Dakota. A hardware store manager fixed my trekking pole that had broken in two (with hard plastic tubing and a lot of duct tape), I charged my electronics at a Chinese restaurant, and the local police gave me permission to set up my tent in the local park.

But as I broke off the highway and began trespassing over farmland once again, the warmth and hospitality of town gave way to a cold and uninviting countryside. It was a weekend and hunters were out, so every few minutes I heard the *putt, putt, putt* of rifle shots. Most of the shots were far away, but there were a few sharp bangs from nearby that felt so close I found myself looking at my limbs to make sure I hadn't been shot and had been walking purely on pain-numbing adrenaline. In one rocky section, I heard gunfire so close that I dove behind a rock and waved my new orange hunting vest in the air as if it were a white flag of surrender. When a covey of quail rocketed out of some shrubbery, my heart stopped.

This wasn't ideal land to be trespassing over, unlike the endless grasslands of Alberta and Montana. There, I'd walked for hours before seeing an abandoned home or a gravel road. I'd felt so unobserved that I'd drop my pants and go to the bathroom as unabashedly as the cows. But here there was a vast network of country roads, each separated by a mile, with many small family-run farms growing corn and sunflowers (which had been harvested months before). Every time I leaped over a fence, I felt as if I were being watched, or that I might accidentally walk into someone's backyard upon mounting a hill. I hopped a barbed-wire fence, and when I looked back, I spotted a red truck prowling behind me. I waved, but all that was returned was a blank glare.

On the road, a landowner who owned a dump saw me walking. He was the sort who looked like he'd been battered by an addiction and buoyed by religion—a rescued dog, bearing a renewed faith in humanity from kind treatment, but in the depths of him still lurked the monster of his past who might snap at someone's hand whether extended out of kindness or malice.

"I'm on a long walk," I said.

"You're fucking crazy, man," he said.

"Well," he said, reconsidering, "I guess you gotta do something. Me, I run this dump. And about four hundred head of cattle. I get in trouble if I'm not doing something."

I asked him if I was in Nebraska yet, and he said that the state was just past the line of evergreens. Careful not to walk on his property or in his woods, I took the road into Nebraska.

It was cold and the sun was hidden behind an overcast sky. Because I didn't have the directional aid of the sun and because I was nervous about the last guy and the red truck, I walked due west—in the wrong direction—for an hour.

I crossed the South Dakota–Nebraska border around dusk and staggered into the town of Mills. The town, like many country towns in these areas, was hardly a "town" in the conventional sense of the word. There weren't any businesses, only about six homes, half of which seemed deserted. I called out hello in front of one but was greeted only by a sleepy dog. There was a building—the town's community center and history museum—that had a truck parked in front of it. I knocked on the door and no one answered, but I heard a vacuum purring inside, so I sat on my pack on the front lawn waiting for them to finish. Another truck pulled up and a large man in his seventies wearing a camo-patterned shirt got out and, amused, asked, "Well, what might you be doing in Mills?"

I told him about my expedition and asked where I could set up camp for the night. He said his name was Gary and that I could set up my tent in the woods by the creek. But first, he brought me into the museum for a tour. The museum, which Gary runs, used to be a home. It's still fully furnished and operational, serving as a sort of hunting hostel during the fall and also as a museum for the locals in the area who'd given Gary their family histories and photo albums.

Gary showed me around. I looked at all the pictures on the walls. Many were family pictures or pictures of kids lined up in front of their school from the 1930s and '40s. "Mechanization has changed the way of life here. When I was a boy, there were four schools within twenty miles. Now there's one high school with thirty kids."

We sat at the kitchen table, and we talked, or Gary talked and I listened. He told me about his twenty-eight years as a county commissioner, his son's ranch down south, and the few times he lobbied in Washington for a farming program.

"When you get older, you get more opposed to change," he said about himself. He's appalled that the Ten Commandments can't be displayed in government buildings, he's scared to death about the influx of foreign-exchange students for fear of another terrorist attack (that might take place in Omaha, Nebraska, where the U.S. Strategic Command is based), and he's doubtful that climate change has been influenced by mankind, claiming that the temperature was just as warm during Lewis and Clark's expedition across the region two hundred years ago.

I listened carefully, keeping all of my thoughts to myself. I didn't say anything, but I was taken aback and somewhat unsettled by how different our concerns were. We got along well enough, though, and he offered me the museum for the night, along with all its amenities, and whatever food I'd like to forage from the fridge and cupboards.

He left for home, and I had a *Risky Business* moment in my thermal underwear on the kitchen's linoleum floor, jubilantly sliding across it. *Man, I'm going to enjoy this.*

I started with a long steaming-hot shower, periodically nudging the shower dial closer and closer to the *H*, and soon enough I was bathing in a fog of sizzling steam. I shampooed my hair twice, my beard once, scrubbed my armpits, and thoroughly cleaned between my toes. I threw my clothes into the washing machine, and while wearing my black thermal underwear, I made a supper of lima beans, tater tots, and ground beef, all retrieved from the freezer. I turned on the Sunday night Packers-Giants game, watching it while stitching up my torn clothes, which had become a once-a-week ritual.

The house felt as if it had been broken in well, as if good lives had been lived there. There were awkward-looking family pictures from the 1990s, shelves of books with 1950s bindings, a rifle mounted on two deer hooves. Oh, the domestic bliss! I felt as if I could have spent a whole week here, happily sleeping next to the propane heater, watching stupid television shows, concocting strange dinners from the food that visiting hunters had left, and playing Minesweeper on their ancient computer.

I walked down the halls of the museum late in the night, looking at the pictures of families from the 1930s and '40s. The people looked young and strong and thin. I wondered if a place such as Mills—and all the abandoned towns I'd walked through—would have been better off without the mechanized industry that made these families, with their sturdy bodies and tough hands, unnecessary and obsolete. I thought I'd be happier in a village with good homemade food, close neighbors, and laughing children than in an empty one where one man and a few John Deeres can handle six thousand acres. But I suppose it's easy to get nostalgic about the past, especially one you hadn't lived. Perhaps, in my reverie, I'd failed to take into account the aching backs, the workdays from sunup till sundown, the dead infants, the dairy cows gone dry.

"It was all hard labor," Gary had said.

. . .

I n the morning, I watched *The Today Show* as I ate my breakfast and packed up. There was an inch of snow on the ground, and I wasn't at all eager to leave my little warm home.

I walked over prairie, hopping over fences rather than rolling under them so as not to let the wet snow moisten my clothes. I kept on Highway 137 even though it didn't follow the pipeline because I wanted to use the bridge to cross the potentially uncrossable Niobrara River.

A thirtysomething man in a small SUV pulled over to me and asked me why I was walking.

"I'm about to make some lunch," he said. "Do you want to come over for some?"

I walked a half mile back to his home, which seemed both local (with its mounted heads of deer and camo bedspreads) and worldly (with a shiny keyboard placed in front of a big Mac computer monitor). While Stan made a watermelon smoothie and grilled cheese on pumpernickel, and offered me zucchini bread, still moist, that his mom had made him, I filled him in on my adventure. The XL, it turned out, is set to go through his land, which he's okay with because of the compensation he'll receive and because he acknowledges that we have an oil-dependent economy.

"But don't even think about going on my neighbor's land," he warned. I thought this was going to be another Great Plains tough-guy boast, but apparently his neighbor was so upset about the XL going through his property that he'd taken his gun out and threatened the TransCanada land agents who had tried to cross his land.

"He'll really shoot you," Stan said.

"Say no more," I said. "I'll stay off."

I thought Stan and I were similar. We were close in age, it seemed he'd been to college, and he had an appreciation for the beauty of the prairie, which I'd come to admire, too. Unlike my conversations with older folks who prefer to talk more than listen, my conversation with Stan was far more of a give-and-take. I'd been hoping to meet someone like him: someone I could ask provocative questions without worry of causing offense; someone who might give me a clearer understanding of the Great Plains mind-set.

"Are people around here concerned about global warming?" I asked.

"No," he said, with a surprised smile. "Why? Are you?"

"I'm definitely worried that we're warming our planet," I said.

Stan said he was happy I was there because he never got to talk to people like me and that I might be able to fill in some of his blind spots. He said that the people in this area are independent, hardworking, self-reliant, and that they resent any sort of government interference. He told me that the government asked some of the ranchers to build fences around their canyons so their cows couldn't defecate in the Niobrara River. He also said that the government was spending tens of millions of dollars studying a bug that might be affected by the pipeline (which, I'd later learn, wasn't true, as the research was a free service provided by a few professors and students from a local university). I was doubtful about the bug thing, as I didn't think a narrow pipeline would have a huge impact on a whole species, but what did I know? Perhaps there was an unreasonably expensive study, but without that knowledge, I couldn't disagree with him.

He said he thought global warming was all "hype," created so the government could seize more power.

"We can take care of our own land," he said. "We don't need the government to come here and tell us how to live." Environmentalism, as he saw it, was more or less a ploy for more government control.

"Don't you think environmentalism is all about power?" he asked.

I was stunned silent by the question. It was now clear that we had such different values, such different ways of thinking. My mind went in a hundred directions at once, giving me no clear rhetorical path to follow. Environmentalism, to me, had nothing to do with power. Environmentalism was about stopping another Love Canal from happening. It was about keeping fracking away from my old North Carolina home. It was about keeping the Gates of the Arctic National Park wild and undeveloped. It was about giving caribou calving grounds, eating foods from healthy soil, and making our planet habitable for the next seven generations. To me, environmentalism was about, well, life. And to be opposed to it was so unthinkable that my mind had no response prepared and could not improvise one on the spot. From the phrasing of this one question, I gathered that any sort of mutual understanding was impossible.

Antienvironmentalism and climate change denial are no strangers to the Great Plains. But denial, of course, is not exclusive to the Heartland. It seems that the more temperature records are broken, the more the sea level rises, and the more destructive our storms get, the more we as a country try to put climate change out of our minds. For the first time since 1988, climate change was not brought up in any presidential debates. Of twenty countries polled, America ranks at the top of countries that are doubtful about the existence of climate change. According to a Pew Research Center poll, only 18 percent of Romney's supporters believed in man-made climate change and only 25 percent of Tea Party Republicans agreed that global warming, man-made or not, is happening. Meanwhile, in the real world, 97 percent of climate scientists acknowledge man's role—a consensus Galileo would have killed for.

But because a warming planet is so frightening and the prospect of changing one's lifestyle so unsettling, people force themselves to believe it isn't true. When there isn't outright denial, there's apathy. The Greek *apatheia* means the refusal or inability to experience pain. When you don't want to or don't know how to deal with the pain of climate change, apathy becomes an attractive alternative. And it's hard to blame the deniers for it. Living in ignorance or apathy, after all, might be more sensible than living in fear.

The plains weren't always this way. In the early 1900s, they were a hotbed of progressivism, granting women the right to vote well before most all of the states east of the Mississippi. Because of the difficult nature of making a living on the plains, the people became, according to Wallace Stegner, "militantly cooperative, even socialistic." In Kansas—now one of the most conservative states—was a town called Radical City. Nearby, in Girard, Kansas, the socialist newspaper *Appeal to Reason* was printed and read by hundreds of thousands. There, in 1908, Eugene V. Debs accepted the Socialist Party's nomination for president.

But eventually the people were either defeated by Dust Bowls, made obsolete by technology, or grew rich from oil. And the progressivism—and all that pioneer fervor—vanished.

The Heartland now beats with a dull thump. Take a drive through the plains and you'll see ghost towns, barns rotting, barbed wire rusting on old wooden posts. I never saw children, and the women of child-bearing age seem to have vanished from the face of the prairie as dramatically as the buffalo. The few men my age crowd around slot machines in bars. Hunting excursions take place more behind steering wheels than on foot. Earlier, I happened upon a group of farmers at a diner playing gin, and they teased the big guy at the table, saying that he liked to go on long walks, too. "From the couch to the TV," he said, laughing.

And now there is a foreign corporation that wants to jam a thirty-six-inch-diameter pipe through the land their great-grandfathers homesteaded, and no one seemed to think that there was anything wrong with it. Where was the Wild West unrest, the cowboy chivalry, the calls for rebellion?

I came here to see the center of the universe, but at times, the Heartland seemed like the farthest thing from it. Maybe the hot, the passionate, and the ambitious don't suit this land anymore. Maybe there's nothing wrong with taking over the land your great-grandpa homesteaded and living a quiet life on the farm. Maybe, but I thought there was something missing. There's a heavy contentment with the everyday task, but where's the exuberance of the uncommon deed?

My speechlessness with Stan was slow to break, and what words came out were garbled and mostly incoherent. The subject was changed and we awkwardly said good-bye, both of us maintaining our good humors. I walked down the highway, careful not to step on his neighbor's land (which had a threatening sign on it that read THIS PROPERTY IS GOVERNED BY THE CASTLE DOCTRINE).

I crossed the bridge over the Niobrara River, hopped a fence, and continued southeast through the Nebraska prairie.

13.

The Deputy

December 7, 2012

←→

I n Atkinson, Nebraska, at the local library, I bumped into Cindy Myers, an RN from nearby Stuart. She'd voted Republican all her life but had become disillusioned with the party and its gung-ho stance on the XL, which she thought threatened her and many other Nebraskans' drinking water.

This was the person I'd wanted to meet all along: a red-state radical, furious and determined. Myers's family drinks pure groundwater from the Ogallala Aquifer, which sits beneath 174,000 square miles across seven states and much of Nebraska, providing water for 27 percent of the irrigated farmland in the United States and 82 percent of the drinking water for those who live atop it.

"Water is more valuable than gold to me," said Myers. "It's more valuable than oil. I just felt in my heart that it was my responsibility to do something."

Like many Nebraskans, Myers became outspoken about the XL

when she heard that the pipe and its dirty oil would flow through her groundwater. After Nebraskans voiced their concerns, TransCanada proposed an alternative route, but the XL was still set to run through a ninety-mile stretch of the aquifer, where the water table is less than fifty feet beneath the surface.

Myers was preparing to testify at a hearing in Albion, Nebraska, on December 4. She told me there would be hundreds in attendance, anti-XL rallies, and impassioned testimonies. "You need to get to Albion, Ken," she said. "It's going to be big."

I spent the afternoon drying out my saturated tent on the lawn in front of the library while I spoke with Cindy inside. Every morning, the tent would be coated in frost crystals, but in the afternoon, when the sun would heat up my pack, the tent would turn sodden and need to be dried out.

In the evening, I went to the town bowling alley, where I out-ate everyone at the pizza buffet. Bob Seger blared from speakers, and balls crashed into pins. One of the waitresses, Deneen, sat down and chatted with me, telling me about her three girls and small-town life.

Deneen seemed taken with me and regretted that her older college-aged daughter wasn't in town.

"I wish Kara was in town!" she said. "You guys would be so good together."

Deneen, who couldn't stomach the thought of me out in the cold, called her pastor to ask if he would let me sleep in the church.

I unrolled my sleeping pad on the floor in a large room where Sunday school lessons were taught. After slipping into my sleeping bag, I began to feel sorry about all the bad things I'd said about Christianity. As someone who loved nature, who thought gay people should have equal rights, and who didn't take kindly to people implying my soul would forever burn in hell just because I didn't believe what they believed, I'd become quite intolerant of the religion.

But on this trip I'd received such kind treatment from the Heartland's many practitioners, and none of them ever asked if I was Christian or tried to convert me. They gave their lawns, floors, and warmth, and expected nothing in return. Earlier, a Jehovah's Witness up in South Dakota, who'd heard about me at a diner I'd stopped in, jumped in his medical-supply vehicle, stormed down the road, found me, and offered any medical supplies I might need. I gladly filled up on rubbing-alcohol wipes and vitamin supplements.

While their views on same-sex marriage and reproductive choice— among other social issues—are often less than tolerant, it was clear that their sense of charity had been heightened. I wondered if some of their rigid social positions might have had more to do with being secluded in a fairly homogenous culture—which they'd been brought up in and had little control over—and less to do with their mostly good-hearted religious teachings.

In the morning, I found notes and chocolates that Deneen's two high school–aged daughters had left me.

Determined to get to Albion in time for the hearing, I continued down the Cowboy Trail, a rails-to-trails bike path that headed east across Nebraska. The Keystone XL was in the process of being rerouted across Nebraska, so I had to find my own way across the state, and the trail was a convenient discovery. It was, though, awfully boring compared to life on the open prairie, where I had daily en-counters with landowners and animals. And because I had nothing to worry about and no sights to enchant me now, I could focus my attention on how much my swollen feet hurt, which made them hurt doubly worse.

I slept in the woods in between farms or on church lawns in the towns I passed through. I turned south down Highway 14, hopping from one small country town to the next. I made it to a town called Petersburg, and I had only twelve more miles left before reaching Albion, where the meeting would take place the next day.

In Petersburg (pop. 333), I was sitting at the counter at a convenience store, which also ran a small Chester's fried-chicken franchise inside. I sat next to a pile of chicken breasts warming under a hot lamp. In front of me were the remains of my lunch: two empty yogurt containers and a banana peel. I'd just finished watching the documentary *Buck*, about a famous horse whisperer, from my friend's Netflix account on my iPad, and I began to upload pictures for a new blog entry.

I felt the presence of something to my left, so I looked over and saw a police officer in a tan uniform. On his chest was a brass, sharp-cornered star. He was probably in his early forties.

"Hello there," I said.

"Can I give you a ride out of the county?" he asked.

"Umm . . . I'm actually on a walking expedition. I'm headed to Texas," I said. (I'd been offered dozens of rides, but I'd politely declined them all, as I was determined to do the whole trip on foot.)

"Well, I need to give you a ride out of the county," he said sternly.

Now what's all this about? I thought.

He asked me what I was doing, and I told him that I was a writer and that I was following the pipeline. When he took my North Carolina driver's license, he asked what my job in North Carolina was. I stumbled a bit with the question, as the whereabouts of my true home and the title of my true job were unclear even to me. Eventually, I said

I'd been a student in North Carolina, where I received my master's degree.

"Hmm . . . a master's degree," he said, even more suspicious.

I began to feel nervous. He was carefully inspecting my every move, looking for any sign of guilt. Aware that my nervousness might be construed as guilt, I became hyper self-conscious, and every physical movement now had layers of thought behind it.

He said he'd explain everything in the car.

We walked to the parking lot, and I said, "Sir, if you want me out of the county, I'd much prefer to walk out. I promised myself that I was going to walk the whole way to Texas. I haven't been in a vehicle for seventy days. If you say I must get in the vehicle, I will. But I'd rather walk."

"You need to get in the vehicle. I have orders to take you out of town."

He opened the door to the backseat, and I stepped in. Behind me, to my left, and in front of me was a hard metal cage.

I wondered what could have caused this. The pipeline path, in this part of Nebraska, closely parallels roads, so for the past week I hadn't done any trespassing. I'd been walking on the shoulders of roads, which is perfectly legal. So surely this wasn't why I was being escorted out of town.

It had been a fairly normal day. I'd been walking south down Highway 14 all morning. I arrived in Petersburg around noon. I aired out my sleeping bag at the park for half an hour and looked for the local library so I could do computer work. The library had been closed, so I went to the convenience store, where I bought a meal and watched *Buck*. I figured I'd hang out there for a bit before heading back to the local campground for a long night of pleasure reading.

Did someone see me looking into the library windows? Or maybe someone thought it was strange that I was airing out my damp sleeping bag at the empty playground? Or maybe a few paranoid passersby called the cops from the road, weirded out by the bearded guy walking along the highway? I wasn't sure what I'd done wrong. Without any other idea, I worried that someone had caught me peeing by an evergreen tree in the previous town when I thought no one was looking. Am I going to end up on one of those *lists*?

He got in the driver's seat and told me that there were reports that two homes had been broken into that afternoon. One homeowner, apparently, had come home and the doors were unlocked. Another family, a few blocks away, had discovered that their dog had been let out of the house.

I pictured Edna walking to her back porch and screaming in a shrill, blood-curdling screech, "Frank . . . Who let the dogs out?!"

"I've been walking for like seventy days," I said to the deputy. "I wouldn't have gotten this far if I'd been breaking into homes along the way."

He took me to the first house that I'd supposedly broken into, and asked, accusingly, like I'd suddenly buckle and confess everything: "Does this look familiar to you?"

It was a small nondescript home about the size of a double-wide.

"No," I said. "I haven't even been on this side of town."

We drove down a few blocks. "You said you got two calls?" I asked, while turning on my camera to audio record the conversation.

"Yepper," he said. He pulled up to the second house.

"And this house right here," he said, pointing to another equally nondescript house. "I hope it wasn't you, and if I find out it was, you'll be coming back to Boone County, Nebraska."

"Well," I said, unable to hold back a chuckle at all this ridiculousness, which reminded me of all of my mother's false accusations throughout my adolescence. "You're free to check my stuff."

Day turned into night as we headed south down Highway 14. I could still vaguely see the rolling land, mostly fallow hay fields and cornfields. I was upset that I was in a vehicle, but for the most part, I was amused by the situation. Here I was, a foreigner being wrongly accused of a crime—the dog liberator—in a small country town. This was all so movielike. So *First Blood*. So *My Cousin Vinny*. The only thing missing was a conversation in which each of us thought we were talking about two different crimes.

"Listen, Officer," I'd say, thinking this was all about my indecently peeing in the woods. "I just had to do it. I didn't think anyone was watching."

"You had to do it?" he'd say.

"Well, it's an impulse, a compulsion . . ."

"So you admit to it?"

"Well, yeah, I admit to it."

"And this wasn't the first time you've done it?" he'd ask.

"Goodness, no," I'd say, taken aback. "I've been doing it in towns all along the way."

He'd nod to himself, as this would confirm all his suspicions.

"Normally, I'm more careful about it," I'd add. "But you gotta go when you gotta go."

"Well, you ain't goin' to be goin' nowhere for a long time, boy. Alls I know is that we're gonna settle this right here in Boone County, Nebraska."

"So how far along is the county line?" I asked.

For the past week, I'd planned to arrive in Albion on December 4. There would be protests, demonstrations, and impassioned testimonies about the Keystone XL route. I'd meet many environmentalists

and landowners opposed to it. It was sure to be a goldmine for information, so I was not at all happy being shipped out of and possibly
banned from Albion.

"You got thirteen miles till you get to Albion," he said. "Then another thirteen to eighteen miles to get out of the county from Albion."

"So does that mean I won't be able to be in Albion tomorrow for
that meeting?"

"Umm . . . probably."

"You mean I probably won't be able to be in town?" I asked.

"Not unless you get yourself back there. Alls I know is that I'm
gettin' you out of my county because of what's happened so far. I can't
prove you did anything wrong, and you're not in any kind of trouble,
but things like that don't happen in a town of only 180 to 220 people.
We don't got no crooks in Petersburg."

"Sir, I don't appreciate your accusatory tone," I said. "I'm a good
person. I've never stolen anything in my life. I think this is wrong."

He coughed, then after a minute of silence, he started to make
small talk about the weather, but I was too upset to indulge him.

For some reason, he couldn't take me the whole way, so he pulled
over in a big gravel lot, where another police officer was parked in his
SUV. He was supposed to take me the rest of the distance. When we
got out, I asked the deputy, "Do you want to go through my pack?"

"No, because I don't know if they're missing anything," he said.

He then began to update the other officer.

"We had one report, but with two houses . . . One of the houses
had a dog that was inside the house. Now the dog's outside. No one
else is around. They should be at home. So it leads to suspicion. Can't
accuse him of it, 'cause you can't prove it. So the sheriff just said,
'Move him out.'"

"He's a writer," the deputy continued. "And he's following the pipeline, and he wants to be at tomorrow's meeting. Guess we can't stop him from coming back. At least we're getting him out of the way now."

I was standing only a few feet away as they talked about me this way. Despite the disrespect and accusatory tone, my amusement had returned and I listened to their conversation with an emotion bordering on glee.

The other officer seemed far more levelheaded. As we continued south past Albion, he asked what I was doing. I started from the beginning of my trip—all the way back in Denver—and gave him a thorough description of all the stages of my journey.

"I think this is all so silly," I told him. "*I have an iPad.* It's not like I'm destitute."

This new officer, feeling sorry about the whole thing, turned down a gravel road and made his way back to a campground in Albion, where I'd spend the night.

14.

The Governor

December 11, 2012

←→

The next day, I walked with my backpack and trekking poles into the Boone County Fairgrounds, where the hearing was taking place. Between my near arrest and bedraggled appearance, I began to feel vaguely guilty. I imagined that the drivers in passing cars were eyeing me warily, perhaps thumbing 911 on their cell phones.

When I arrived at the fairgrounds, I noticed STOP THE PIPELINE signs plastered everywhere. A Native-American tribal leader, standing with his family and a small horse, was giving a speech to a throng of protesters in the dark.

I walked into the lobby of the fairgrounds, which was a hornet's nest of Nebraskans who'd come here from all parts of the state to have their say on the pipeline.

"It's the walker!" yelled a woman across the room. The group crowded around me.

I was swarmed, barraged with questions about my hike, given enthusiastic hugs, wholehearted thank-yous, and two women stuffed seventy dollars in my pants. Ranchers brought me buffalo jerky and homemade pepper jack cheese.

What the hell is going on?

Apparently, Cindy, who brought me a jug of delicious pure Ogallala water, had posted a message about my journey on Facebook, and it went viral among XL radicals.

I may have been covered in dust and I may have been able to smell my crotch in a cold breeze, but I walked into the hearing with a straightened back and a raised chin, feeling like a real adventurer.

One-hundred-sixty-seven people signed up to speak, and the hearing went until two a.m. There were union members wearing orange T-shirts that read APPROVE THE KEYSTONE XL PIPELINE SO AMERICA WORKS. Members of Americans for Prosperity, supported by the Koch brothers, came to lend their support for the pipeline. But most of the crowd was made up of farmers, ranchers, and plain old Nebraskans deathly afraid that this pipe might—whether through climate change or contaminated water—destroy their lives.

Over the course of the next six hours, I listened to them speak. There were hoots and hollers and raucous applause. A woman called for rebellion, and an old farmer, grizzled and clad in denim, shuffled up to me, looked me in the eye, and whispered, "That's how we do it in Nebraska."

The next day, I packed up my things, and with the wind at my back and Ogallala in my veins, I continued south toward Kansas.

While Rick Hammond may never have been officially elected to political office, he's known to some as the "governor."

I'd met Rick and his daughter Meghan at the hearing. Eager to help out, they suggested I stop by their home for a meal and some rest.

Rick, a proud veteran of the Peace Corps (and "a liberal in a red state," as he put it) had gone on a consulting trip to Russia years ago, where he'd shared information about raising cattle. Either because of a miscommunication or because the Russian company that had hired him wanted to exaggerate the company's prestige, they introduced Rick to their colleagues as the "ex-governor of Nebraska."

"I'm just a farmer," Rick would say, bewildered.

His guests would laugh, endeared to Rick's modesty. But the company continued to treat him as if he were an illustrious guest. He was assigned a gang of bodyguards. Solemn toasts of vodka were given in his honor. Russian Cossack dancers sought Rick out to have their picture taken with him.

Rick felt guilty about the misunderstanding, so he demanded that his translator stop introducing him as the "governor."

"I was never governor!" Rick repeated.

At the end of his trip, at an important meeting with a large group of men, someone from the audience asked Rick, "How did you become the governor of Nebraska?"

Rick felt all the eyes in the room on him. These admiring men were humbled to be in the presence of this great American leader.

Rick looked at his translator and then to the crowd, and said—with a stately firmness—"Hard work and honesty."

I crossed a bridge over the Platte River and began heading east to meet up with the pipeline, which goes through Rick's family's property. His daughter saw me from her truck and asked if I wanted to toss in my pack. I said sure, and she said Rick would be bringing a pair of horses down the road.

Sure enough, the governor arrived, and I rode a horse for the first time alongside Rick, who, in his cowboy hat and dark shades, held my reins. He took me to his place, where he taught me about cattle, bees, windmills, and a hundred other things about running a ranch. After two shots of vodka from a bottle he'd brought home from Russia, we stumblingly hoisted up his Christmas tree.

With memories of his Peace Corps days in mind, Rick suggested that he join my hike. Even though Rick said he sees himself as a thirty-year-old "swashbuckler," he thought that as a sixty-year-old rancher he could lend some credibility to my hike. Meanwhile, his family, who was mortally opposed to the XL, called up every media source in the area so we could get out our anti-KXL message to a bigger audience. In just the first two days, we were interviewed by two TV news stations and two newspapers.

Our goal for Rick's first day was twenty-four miles to the town of McCool Junction, where he had connections at the church. The day was bright and sunny, but the temperature was a crisp eight degrees Fahrenheit. We set out from his mother-in-law's home, where I'd slept the last couple of nights. After sixteen miles, the sun was setting and Rick's feet were hurting, so we abandoned his church plans, and Rick suggested we head to his friend Chet's ranch. We crossed Chet's land, a cornfield that had been "disced." (Farmers pull behind their tractors an implement called a disc that has rows of spherical blades that slice into cornfields after the harvest to help break down the corn without disturbing the soil too much.) Walking in a deeply plowed field was never pleasant because dust would often get kicked up and blow into my eyes and because it simply took more energy to push through the clumps of dry soil. Disced fields were always more manageable.

We saw Chet ahead, so we happily called out to him, waving our hands and poles in the air, excited about a home where we could rest our feet and cook a meal. Chet, seeing two screaming men walking through his field, did the sensible thing and walked into his house and loaded his gun.

A fter a night at Chet's, who thankfully kept the gun snugly tucked into the back of his pants, we continued on across Nebraska. Rick felt reluctant to trespass over property, so we stuck to roads, which, in this part of the country, all run straight north and south and east and west exactly one mile apart.

As our boots crunched over loose gravel, we swapped tales of past loves, filled each other in on our histories, and grumbled about the XL.

Rick had grown up on a ranch in Curtis, Nebraska, in the southwestern part of the state. After bouncing around a few colleges, where he studied sociology and Russian literature, he joined the Peace Corps and lived in Ecuador for two years. When he got back, he met a farmer's daughter, whom he adored. But Rick still felt drawn to the adventurous life. He wasn't sure whether to stay and build a family or continue to live his life of adventure.

When Rick was twenty-nine, his girlfriend's father asked him, "So, what's the plan, Rick?"

"If we're not married in six months, I'm outta here," Rick said, surprised to hear those words come out of his mouth.

"When two people are in the same point of their life journeys at the same time," Rick said to me, "then love and commitment will easily follow the physical attraction that brought the two together. Sometimes it's as much about timing as it is about being in love. Someday you might want more stability in your life."

When was I going settle down? All of my friends had homes and real jobs. My high school friend Chris was married and had two kids. Josh was married and had a kid on the way.

I liked to think that I was the sort of person who wasn't affected by ridiculous, culturally prescribed expectations of what a person is supposed to have achieved before a certain age. But, for some reason, I was affected by the fact that in about six months the digits of my age would change from two and nine to three and zero.

I'd spent my twenties well: going to college, having adventures, moving around. But how does one spend his thirties well? I'd known people who'd prolonged their twenties into their forties—going on three-month-long trips to Thailand, then working for ten dollars an hour at camp jobs, then going on another trip—and to me, they always seemed to be traveling aimlessly, with neither strong roots set in any place nor much meaning behind their constant wanderings. Yet by no means did I want to enroll in accounting school and abandon the adventurous life I'd been enjoying. Could I keep going on adventures like these forever? Should I double down and focus on a career no matter how unappealing that sounded?

Uncertainties aside, I did know that this hike was what I was supposed to be doing at this point in my life. Here in Nebraska, on the path of the XL, was exactly where I needed to be. I may have had concerns about how to spend my future, but there was no question about how I ought to be spending my present. How rare is it to not want to be somewhere or someone else? How rare is it to have that sense of clarity, that sense that you are exactly where you need to be at this very moment in time? When you're asked what you want to be or do, how many times do you get to say, "Exactly what I'm doing right now"?

I thought I had gotten to this place because I'd trusted that initial flash of inspiration I had felt when Liam suggested we hike the path a year before. In time, all such flashes dim. The potentially life-altering sensation that once felt so ground shaking always goes away, and it's easy to come up with reasons not to follow through. *A bear will maul me. I'll get shot. I just don't know if I can do it.* But I didn't want to let that flash go. I wanted to remember it. I wanted to hold on to it. I wanted to hold on to it because I had a hunch that these flashes come for a reason—perhaps they represent some aching existential need, or perhaps they're paths presented to us by something greater than ourselves, or perhaps they're messages uploaded from the subconscious. I'd learned long ago not to think of those flashes of inspiration as crazy ideas but as messages from fate calling upon you to do something grand.

The tug-of-war between freedom and security, adventure and comfort, voluntary poverty and wealth would always exist in me, just as it did in Rick. I didn't have the answers, but I did know that I would not sacrifice my present to live for the future. The Plains Indians, to survive, didn't sit still in droughts or build permanent townships. They followed the buffalo and the rain. And they were able to survive for thousands of years in an unforgiving land because of this flexibility, this embracing the present without obsessing over the future. Better to be guided by lightning strikes, I thought.

. . .

On our third day together, when we stopped to take a break in a ditch, I grabbed Rick's bedroll and strapped it to my pack.

"Hey, what are you doin'?" Rick asked.

"I've been carrying my pack for so many months I barely feel the weight anymore," I said. "It's no big deal."

"You're pulling me up by my tail," he said.

"By your tail?"

"When we have a calf that's struggling, we help him out. We pull him up by his tail. That's what you're doing for me."

Despite Rick's international experiences, he was at heart a man of the plains, full of practical knowledge and cowboy wisdom. He called horse dung "road apples," taught me about the different species of grasses, and explained the intricacies of growing corn. As it got warmer, instead of saying that he was going to remove a layer of clothing, Rick said, "I gotta shuck some duds."

Some of Rick's explanations about farm equipment were so technical that they went completely over my head, but I was happy to have a local guide, and someone to walk with. I called him the "governor" as a joke, but I saw that Rick did have a bit of the silver-tongued politician in him. He was smooth talking and persuasive and diplomatic. He could be too assertive at times, but he was always genial. He could put anybody at ease.

My lack of knowledge—about everything—became apparent to Rick immediately, so he was determined to teach me everything he could.

When I asked him what a "pivot" is (the watering apparatus that pivots in a circle irrigating crop fields), he took my ignorance almost as a personal offense. When I stopped him in midsentence to ask what a "combine" was (a machine that reaps, threshes, and winnows corn or soybeans), he looked at me with a mix of pity and bewilderment, and said, "Duckling, by the end of this trip, you're going to know a bit more about how the world works."

Rick was still leery of trespassing, so we stayed on roads, which added miles to our trip, but I didn't mind now that I had a companion. But as we continued on, Rick began to realize how much longer we'd have to hike if we stuck to roads. With his heavy pack and sore feet, leaving the roads to reduce our mileage suddenly became an appealing prospect. We were looking at my map and I pointed out our route. "It's 6.5 miles by road," I said, "but about four miles as the crow flies." Rick, whose confident stride had turned into a hobo's hobble, scoffed at the idea of taking roads.

"We'll take the field," he said.

We were now going over corn and grass and soybean fields. In a pasture, upon observing me flinch when a couple of cows trotted past, he exclaimed, "They're not going to hurt you! They're just curious!"

A woman who recognized us as the famous pipeline walkers pulled over in her car and offered to haul our packs to Fairmont. In midoffer, Rick, who didn't even know this woman, tore off his pack and heaved it into her backseat.

A reporter with the *Lincoln Journal Star* came to interview us for a story (in which I'd be unflatteringly, and, dare I say, falsely, called "grimy-looking," as I'd just taken a shower the day before). I sat in the front seat and Rick sat in the back.

The journalist began with the standard question ("Why are you doing this?") and I started giving him my standard answer ("Well, I wanted to go on a long walk"), but as I spoke, I felt Rick's fingers jabbing into my hip. Rick had joined the hike to stir up some publicity in order to fight the pipeline, and he wanted me to get straight to the point and nail TransCanada.

"You don't walk 1,700 miles to go for a stroll," Rick interrupted.

Rick was right. By now, in this reporter's car, I realized that I'd made up my mind and was done holding back.

The jobs, the money, and the oil the pipe would transport—though undeniably beneficial to some people, many of whom I'd met on this trip—did not merit being used as justifications for an industry that is in the process of destroying the planet. The jobs would be few—around five thousand for a couple of years as the pipe is being laid and a mere thirty permanent ones afterward. And despite all the claims that "We need oil!" it may surprise many people to learn that we actually export more oil than we import. In 2011, America's biggest export was fuel. And in 2012 at the refineries at Port Arthur, Texas, where the XL would end, 60 percent of the gasoline and 42 percent of the diesel were exported to foreign countries. Needless to say, much of the tar-sands oil will not end up in our gas tanks and airplanes, as many expect.

But I was never all that interested in the here-and-now details of the XL. Rather, I always thought there was something more to the pipe. Something historic. We've been building pipelines (first in the form of wooden gutters) since the 1860s, yet environmentalists have fought this particular pipeline with unprecedented perseverance. I likened the fight to John Muir's 1906 battle against the damming of Hetch Hetchy Valley, a stretch of protected land in Yosemite National Park that some had called the most beautiful in the world. Never before had Americans united in such numbers to oppose a public-works project for the sake of preserving natural beauty. Muir and the Sierra

Club lost, and the reservoir was built, but from the fight an environmental movement was born. Now, one hundred years later, a similar fight is being waged. This is that moment when a group of people draw a line in the sand and say they've had enough. Regardless of whether the pipeline gets approved or rejected, there seems to be a great change occurring within the country—one that's spelling the end to what has been for more than a hundred years an ordinary source and conveyance of energy.

The solution to humanity's biggest problem still escaped me, but I felt I could say one thing with confidence, especially after traveling one thousand miles on foot: We could get by with far less.

I remembered faltering with CBC a couple of months back when the reporter asked, "Do you think we need this pipeline?" I wished I had said what I would now say to this reporter: "No, I don't think we need this pipeline. We don't need to expand the tar sands. And I don't need this fancy backpack or these trekking poles. I don't even need this trip. North Americans have a funny understanding of the word 'need.' We use twice as much energy per person as Europe. The tar sands emit more CO_2 than many countries. The last thing we need is more oil. We need, rather, different consumption habits, a whole new relationship with the world. We need to quit destroying everything out of a sense of 'need,' when all we really need is a fucking sweater."

Rick and I continued on to Fairmont, where a seventy-year-old woman named Juanita, sympathetic to our cause, had offered to provide us with food, showers, and lodging.

In the morning, Rick and I strapped on our packs and walked along a railway, which Rick was excited about because, as a younger man, he'd worked as an assistant boss on railroads. A photographer for the *Lincoln Journal Star* came to photograph us for the story. He talked about different angles for pictures, mentioning the "watering apparatus" in the background. Rick and I gave each other mirthful looks, just barely managing to contain our ridicule.

"Did you hear what he called the pivot?" I said to Rick later. "A *watering apparatus . . .*"

Eventually, the railroad ended, but there was a path where an extension of the railroad once was, and we walked that for the rest of the day, ducking under branches and climbing down steep slopes where bridges used to be.

"I'm wavering," Rick said, mounting a slope.

Rick had hoped to go all the way to Steele City with me—at the Nebraska-Kansas border—but it was clear that the three days of walking were taking a toll on him.

Then came the dreaded silence of a hiking partner. It's good when they bitch and moan: That means there's still a bit of fight left in them. But when your partner becomes silent, you know he's made his decision, and it's only a matter of time before the expedition party splits.

Rick's sister-in-law Abbi came to the town of Milligan, where we had ended up that night. Rick treated us all to dinner. "I gotta husk some duds," I said in the restaurant.

"You mean shuck," Rick said.

"Well, actually, you're right," he added. "You're learning, duckling."

Rick and I hugged good-bye, and we both very sincerely expressed hope that this wouldn't be our last meeting.

In the morning, I continued on, still following the abandoned railroad path, feeling, for the first time on my long journey, the curious and sharp pang of loneliness.

15.

The Stranger

December 22, 2012

←→

After leaving Rick, I bought some chips and guacamole at the bar in Steele City, just north of the Nebraska-Kansas border. The bartender offered me Steele City's town hall for the night, which was undergoing restoration and serving as a garage for three motorcycles. The jukebox still worked, so I put Bob Marley's "Three Little Birds" on a loop for an hour while lying in my sleeping bag on the couch.

In Nebraska, I'd been a celebrity. I was interviewed by countless small newspapers, the Nebraska chapter of the Sierra Club, NPR, and two TV stations. I was given presents of food and water, and money was stuffed in my pants. Several drivers were, dare I say, "starstruck," pulling over when they spotted me on the side of the road. "I can't believe it's you," said one driver, when I was lying on the grass taking a break. "I mean, I was just out for a drive. And there you are!"

But when I crossed the border into Kansas, it was as if I suddenly turned back into an anonymous bum.

Within minutes, a father and daughter pulled over in their car, and the father asked, "What are you, a . . . a . . . a . . . transient?"

I was walking straight south through Kansas, taking a country road that paralleled the 2010 Keystone Pipeline, which had been laid into Kansas ground a couple of years before. I'd be able to parallel the Keystone till Cushing, Oklahoma, where the second part of the XL would be laid from Cushing to the Gulf Coast of Texas.

Because the Keystone runs almost straight south rather than southeast, I could parallel the pipe on country roads rather than walking fields and hopping a fence every ten minutes, which to me sounded unadventurous, but at least this would give me a nice break from trespassing and cows.

It had rained the previous night, so the dirt road I walked along had turned into soft custardy mud. With each step, my boots sucked up mud that would cling to my soles in sloppy clumps, sometimes curling over the toe like the floppy tips of Oompa-Loompa shoes. At times, it felt as if I were carrying an extra ten pounds on each foot. I got off the road and walked over pasture and wheat fields, which were just beginning to sprout blades of dark green grass.

Kansas was not the flat plain I'd imagined but an endless undulation of gently rolling, up-and-down, tree-topped hills. Like southeastern Nebraska, the roads here are spaced a mile apart, and almost all of the land is developed cropland or pasture.

While I missed the desolateness of those wide-open, half-wild spaces from up north, I found that I'd become less discriminating about nature as I continued south. I needed neither mountains, nor ocean monsters, nor endless prairie to dazzle me. I reminded myself that every field has 4.5 billion years of history in it. Every drop of oil that would flow through this pipeline has been on an epic thousand-mile, million-year journey. There's a story behind every building, pipeline, and person. That tree line is there because of an ambitious FDR-led Great Plains Shelterbelt program instituted during the Great Depression. That corn row was planted by a futuristic GPS-guided tractor. That pile of dirt was once a screaming heap of space-traveling stardust and now perhaps holds the dung of dinosaurs, the slavers' blood of Bloody Kansas, and the chemicals of Big Ag. With a little perspective, the mundane can appear miraculous, and something as unimposing as a field of winter wheat becomes a hidden universe, harboring a history with endless layers of complexity, rendering what on the surface seemed simple to the eye into a bottomless mirror of the cosmos. I figured there was enough wonder in a handful of Kansas soil to keep me marveling for a century.

The winter remained unseasonably warm—with highs in the low fifties—so I walked in as much comfort as I could ask for. I could hear birds again, which, after hundreds of miles of wind, cold, and snow, made my heart swell with thankfulness. I listened to them chirp from thickets, flitting from branch to branch. Out in the open, I watched squadrons of them jubilantly skim the tops of harvested cornfields.

Around dusk, I veered off the road and headed toward a patch of woods, where I set up my tent and cooked a meal of ramen noodles, powdered mashed potatoes, olive oil, and Parmesan cheese all mixed together in a warm and surprisingly tasty calorie-dense mush. Sitting alone in the dark in the woods all by myself, I realized that my journey was approaching its end. *I will miss all of this*, I thought—the interactions with strangers; the simple joys of camping; the occasional suspenseful thrill; the never knowing what's behind the next bend in the road or beyond the next hilltop.

Where do they all go? The books, the lessons, the conversations, the kisses, the dreams? Has everything I've experienced been filed away for safekeeping, each memory ready to fire back to life like a smoldering coal torched by a gust of wind? Or are these experiences more like snowflakes melting on a fingertip: there and pretty one second, and gone forever the next? Will this old barn, this house, those rolling fields, this warble of meadowlarks, and the feelings they evoke be gone forever after I finish? As soon as they'd come, I'd feel them begin to leave. How I wanted to take them all with me. To have them when I'd need them most.

It seems that when you go on a long walk—when you're taking in a constant stream of stimuli—the brain must unload heaps of memories, sometimes expunging experiences from your mind as soon as they come in. My days began to indistinguishably blend into one another. I struggled to recall ordinary words and terms ("carpal tunnel"). Years of coursework were vanishing from my memory banks, leaving me in a state of quiet and simple though increasingly dim-minded peace.

Because you can't take anything with you from the places you pass through—the sights especially—there may be nothing more impermanent than a long walk. Unlike normal domestic living, life on a long walk is not one of material accumulation but of extreme possessionlessness, where the prospect of carrying more things and adding more weight is unthinkable. And it's not just things that you can't add and carry with you but thoughts and ideas and memories, too. You have this sight, this feeling, this breath of wind on your face one moment, and it's gone the next. It's thousands of minutes and miles of instantaneous impermanence, vexing and liberating at the same time.

. . .

In the morning, I continued on to the town of Chapman, where I hoped to charge my electronics and enjoy some of the other luxuries of town: perhaps a church floor or a pint of chocolate ice cream.

Kansas, though, hadn't been giving me the warmest of welcomes up until this point. In my first three days of hiking across the state, I'd been approached by four to five officers (I'd lost count), who'd gotten calls from people worried about my walking with my beard and backpack down their rarely traveled roads. In just a couple of days, I'd had my ID checked more times than I had in all the other states and provinces combined. But it wasn't just the cops (who were all really nice, actually). Oftentimes my waves to drivers weren't returned. Dogs, which had yet to be a problem on this trip, would sprint from their homes and snarl at my heels. These were Labradors from hell: red-eyed and savage. A giant pit bull, chained to its doghouse, lunged at me over and over again. An obese woman in sweatpants came out to yell at the dog. I waved at her twice, but she just stared blankly at me.

I made my way into Chapman and headed straight to the Methodist church. There was no one at the church, so I asked an old man walking a dog where the pastor lived. "My name's Harold Bray," he said, shaking my hand. "I'll take you to his home." Harold was a retired music teacher who plays the trumpet and volunteers for an organization that supplies hotels with Gideon Bibles. We must have looked like an odd couple walking through the middle of Chapman: a ragged, bearded backpacker and Harold, dapper and dignified, with a tiny dog at the end of a leash.

Suddenly, three cop cars converged on us at once. It was a coordinated sting.

Well, this is a bit excessive, I thought.

Two cops got out, one wearing a smile and the other a steely glare. At this point, I was right behind the pastor's house, and I was conscious of how being surrounded by cops wasn't helping me to make the best first impression on Harold or the pastor inside.

Harold, who I'd already thought was one of the kindest, sweetest men I'd ever met, seemed taken aback by the cops, as if he were being targeted as an accomplice for my crimes. "I was just taking him to the pastor's house," Harold explained.

I told them what I was doing and asked one of the officers if he'd like to see my ID.

"You probably have this happen to you all the time, huh?" asked the nice officer, taking my North Carolina license from my outstretched hand.

"Not until Kansas, actually," I said. The cop mentioned something about the most recent school shooting that took place earlier that week (the Newtown, Connecticut, massacre, where a gunman killed twenty schoolchildren and six staff members) and how no one can be trusted these days.

I'd received mostly kindness and generosity on this trip—and that's definitely true—but some of that had to do with what I was: a white, straight, American male in my twenties with nothing particularly unusual about my speech or appearance, minus the beard and backpack. Yet even as a white, twentysomething, straight American (who could easily have been thought to be Christian and conservative as well), I'd been ID'd nearly every day of my walk through Kansas. I was approached by paranoid Montana men and kicked out of Boone County, Nebraska. If it's this hard for me—a Caucasian walking through homogenous Caucasian country—what would it be like if I were black, or gay, or Korean, or Muslim, or a woman, or all of the above?

The pastor wasn't home, so Harold took me back to his place, where he introduced me to his wife, whom he called Saint Maralee.

"Your mother must be worried sick," said Maralee.

"I think she's used to me doing stuff like this," I said.

"No," said Patty, a friend of Maralee's. "She's just putting on a good front. Mothers don't get used to something like this."

"You can tell her," said Maralee, "that now you have two more mothers worried about you."

They fed me chili and let me spend the night at their home. Patty was embarrassed by the local police, so she called the next town I was headed to in order to make sure I'd get a better reception. She gave me a phone number for the town's ex-mayor, Don. I called Don and he told me that I could have the town's Ladies' Lounge for the night.

The Ladies' Lounge?

The very name of the place sent excited shivers up my spine. I pictured a large matronly woman welcoming me into a velvety room cloudy with opium haze and smelling of an anything-goes carnal stink. Along the walls, women with bored expressions would be fanning themselves in aging pastel corsets.

I walked another twenty miles and got to the town of Hope. There were no ladies in the lounge: only Don, a shelf full of books, and a few wicker chairs.

I was grateful, of course, especially since there was supposed to be a blizzard that night.

I stepped outside at midnight and felt so thankful that I had a warm room all to myself. Thick, heavy, wet snowflakes zipped across the street diagonally under the streetlamps. I shuddered, shut the door, and crept into my sleeping bag next to the hot-to-the-touch radiator.

In the morning, Don brought me a breakfast of pizza and chocolate milk, and he told me he'd called the mayor of the next town, where I'd be able to sleep at their senior citizens' center.

Because the road heading straight south was icy and relatively busy, I moved a mile to the west so I could head down a dirt road, where I was sure I wouldn't be struck by skidding vehicles.

After a few miles of walking, I saw a dark figure in the distance walking toward me through this white barren landscape.

Seeing someone else out here was unusual for several reasons. First of all, it was rare to see *anyone* out for a walk. Second, this was yet another remote part of the state, with maybe one house for every mile of road. Third, it was a cold day, with biting twenty-mile-per-hour winds. *Who'd walk in this?* Parts of the road were covered in a foot of snow. And last, this was a black man coming toward me in a part of the country that is almost 100 percent white.

What the hell is he doing walking out here?

I moved to the right side of the road to give him a clear passageway to my left, yet in whatever direction I went, he went. As he came closer, my curiosity gave way to confusion and fear.

He was a young African-American man wearing baggy gray sweatpants and a sweatshirt.

"Good afternoon," I said.

"Do you have a phone?" he asked cheerlessly.

I said no. I did have a phone, but it had stopped working nearly two months ago. (I'd learn later that that wasn't true—I'd merely confused the mute symbol with the no connection symbol; it had been working the whole time.) Plus, my iPad was out of cellular data for the month. While it was true that I thought I had no functioning communication equipment, I think in hindsight that I answered his question more out of impulse than deliberation. For some reason, I suddenly became protective of my gear. All I wanted was to keep walking my way and let him walk his. *What the hell is he doing out here?*

He gave me a disgusted look, and said, "My car slid off the road."

I'd just passed two homes, so I suggested he approach one of them to ask for help.

As I continued on, I became doubtful about his story. Why would he take this dirt road that hasn't been plowed and is never driven on—even when there's no snow—when there is a plowed and perfectly good asphalt highway, surely leading to his destination, a mile to the east? And why didn't *he* have a cell phone?

But sure enough, a mile down the road, I saw his car stuck in hard, crunchy, foot-high snow, and I felt sick to my stomach. I was disgusted with myself. Was there anything I could have done for him? Could I have offered to help push it out? Maybe I should have explained my phone situation better so he didn't think I was some small-minded xenophobe or racist. All along my journey, I'd been looked upon as a transient, a bum, and even as a criminal, yet I discovered that, even with these experiences, I was just as quick to misjudge, to fear the unusual, and to be governed by unexamined and deeply rooted prejudices.

I never found out if he ever got his car out of the snow or if he was just passed along to the next house, and the house after that, by other scared people.

I resolved to be quick to forgive those who'd misjudged me and never let my first instinct—the next time I came across a person in need—be mistrust or fear, but instead to extend the trust and charity that had been shown to me again and again.

16.

The Dog

December 25, 2012

←→

Earlier, on my first day in Kansas, I had walked a country road to the medium-size town of Washington.

A large man was walking with two mammoth Saint Bernards. The Saint Bernards ran up to me, and I asked their owner where I might find a spot in town to set up my tent. He asked me what I was doing, and I asked him what the people in town thought of the pipeline.

"Well, there are pros and cons," he said. "People are pretty upset about the exemption."

"The exemption?"

"Yeah. For some reason, Kansas decided to give TransCanada a ten-year exemption. That means TransCanada don't have to pay no property taxes. We were the only state to do that."

"So what are the pros?" I asked.

"Well . . ." he said, pausing to think. "I guess there aren't any."

An exemption? That made no sense to me. The 2010 Keystone

Pipeline goes through ten states and provinces, yet Kansas was the only one to give them an exemption. All the other states tax pipelines and make millions of dollars from those taxes. That's why states like pipelines: They get money from them.

Kansas experienced a series of lucrative oil strikes in the early twentieth century, but the state is far from the oil giant it once was. The state legislature, attempting to attract new business and revive an old industry, has, in this case, tried to lure companies with desperate incentives.

I walked through the flat fields of Kansas, where old, rusted "nodding donkeys," or pump jacks, stood frozen in time—reminders of the state's irretrievable oil-happy past.

The Kansas economy—and the Plains' economy in general, especially its agricultural industry—was unsustainable then, just as it is today.

Due to the lack of annual precipitation, the plains have always been ill suited for farming. There were severe droughts in 1910, 1917, 1933–1940, the mid-1950s, and the late 1980s, yet the twentieth century may have been the wettest century in two thousand years. (Fossil records show that droughts in the plains have lasted for up to three hundred years!)

Early American homesteaders cashed in on the wet seasons and hunkered down through the bad, deceiving themselves into believing common bromides such as "Rain follows the plow" or "Every dry spell ends with a rain." They hoped electrical currents running through the new railroad tracks and telegraph lines would trigger thundershowers. Tax credits were given to families who planted trees because it was believed that moisture would be driven upward through the branches into the sky. In 1891, in Midland, Texas, the Department of Agriculture funded an experiment to create rain in which Major R. G. Dyrenforth essentially carpet bombed the sky using explosive balloons and kites filled with sulfuric acid, hydrogen gas, and potassium chlorate.

In the 1920s, the price of wheat went down, debts rose, and hard-pressed farmers plowed as much of the native buffalo grass as they could. The rain never came, but the winds did, picking up the bare, parched soil and turning it into 10,000-foot-high, 350-million-ton dirt storms that the locals called "black blizzards," which would plague the plains for much of the 1930s. They were, according to historian Donald Worster, the "most severe environmental catastrophe in the entire history of the white man on this continent." The soil was never the problem. It was rich in nutrients and perfect for crops. But without water, the crops wouldn't grow, and the dry upturned soil would be whisked away by heavy winds.

The Ogallala Aquifer, as mentioned earlier, spreads out underneath eight Great Plains states from South Dakota to Texas. The aquifer contains three billion acre-feet of water (an acre-foot is the amount of water that it takes to cover one acre to the depth of one foot, so the Ogallala, theoretically, could cover all of Canada plus the states of Alaska, California, and Oregon in a foot of water). Because the plains get so little rain (less than an inch of which annually makes it down to refill the aquifer), the aquifer is being used up far faster than nature can refill it. Farmers use 19 million acre-feet a year, and 9 percent of the aquifer has been depleted since the 1950s. According to the National Academy of Sciences, Kansas has already depleted 30 percent of its share of the aquifer.

Plains farming is considered unsustainable because of the arid climate, the dust storms, and farmers' intemperate guzzling of the Ogallala, but the most telling sign of the unsustainable nature of plains farming may be the farmers' long history of depending on government aid. From 1933 to 1939, the plains received one billion dollars from federal programs. This relief, over the years, became an entitlement that plains farmers expected and demanded after all ensuing droughts. In 1988, four billion dollars of federal money was dished out, mostly to the Dakotas, much of it to farmers, many of whom fraudulently claimed wind, rain, and hail damages. "Great Plains farmers," says Worster, "are unique only in the great extent of their dependency." Even though the plains are staunchly red states whose inhabitants complain about big government and entitlements, many of the people in this region are essentially welfare farmers. Of all farms in the country, 33 percent receive government payments, but on the plains, 55 percent do. The nation spends twenty billion dollars a year in direct crop subsidies, almost all of which goes to the states between the Rockies and the Mississippi River. If Montana didn't receive federal subsidies, author Richard Manning reports that the state's net farming income would be zero.

Despite the natural limits of plains farming, it will likely continue to intensify as long as there's aquifer water, fossil fuels, and government aid. When prices for crops rise and farmers can make a bigger profit, they don't hesitate to cut down old tree lines that functioned as wind breaks or turn marginal farmland (usually only good for cattle pasture) into fields of corn and soybean. Between 2006 and 2011, farmers in the Corn Belt (the Dakotas, Nebraska, Minnesota, and Iowa) turned 1.3 million acres of grassland (about the size of Delaware) into corn and soybeans because of what Nebraskans call "seven-dollar corn." It's the biggest ongoing ecological crisis that no one knows about.

As I'd learn on my walk, an undisturbed grassland is an incredible thing. The plains boast of almost twelve dozen species of grass, such as the big blue stem, which can grow ten feet high. The plains grasses, unlike the crops that have replaced them, have evolved to survive droughts and low precipitation, and are perfectly suited to live on the plains. The grasses' narrow blades are ribbed with ridges and covered in hairs that protect them from drying winds. Some grasses know to roll up their leaves in dry spells to keep their tissue moist. But they mostly avoid the scorching sun by living underground, the roots typically making up 60 to 80 percent of the plant's weight. In dry spells, the roots store sugars and proteins as they wait for the next rainfall.

These root-dense soils are home to 60 to 90 percent of all the biological activity in the Great Plains, an underground biosphere that is heavier than the mass of all the animals aboveground. There, too, the native prairie abounds in biodiversity. In the mixed grasslands of the north, a Nature Conservancy study listed 72 mammal species, 18 reptiles, 13 amphibians, 160 butterflies, 222 birds, and 1,595 grasses, sedges, and wildflowers.

What will the plains look like in fifty years? In five hundred? Plains residents won't always have the aquifer to water their crops or the fossil fuels to power their machinery. What's going to happen when the government can no longer justify propping up an unprofitable industry? What happens when everyone leaves? The answers to these questions are significant, not just to the plains but to a nation very much dependent on its breadbasket.

In 1987, two New Jersey academics, Deborah and Frank Popper, tried to answer these questions. The Poppers recognized the inevitable demise of the plains economy and the "largest, longest-running agricultural and environmental miscalculation in American history." Their proposed solution was the "Buffalo Commons," a 139,000-square-mile buffalo sanctuary spread across the plains states, which the Poppers said could be "the ultimate national park" and the "world's largest historic preservation project." They imagined the government helping to return the land to its pre-European state. Not only would the reintroduction of buffalo have ecological benefits but, the Poppers argued, the Commons would also allow portions of the plains to reinvent themselves as ecotourism hotspots.

The Poppers, unsurprisingly, were not exactly given the key to the plains towns they visited. Residents took offense to the Poppers' vision of a plains without people. For them, the Poppers' idea was a tacit condemnation of their livelihoods. Police had to chaperone the Poppers on their visits, and a talk in Montana in 1992 had to be canceled because of death threats.

Over time, however, the Buffalo Commons became more and more real as NGOs, states, private groups, and tribes began to slowly bring the buffalo back. This wasn't the federal government takeover that the Poppers originally envisioned but a scattering of ranchers and groups coming to grips with the challenges of mainstream plains agriculture and seeing the wisdom in bringing back an animal that had evolved to thrive on the plains. The last free-range buffalo was killed in 1891 when there were only a few hundred captives living on ranches. Now there are 500,000 buffalo living in North America, some for reasons of conservation (about 20,000), but most for meat production. According to the USDA's Livestock Slaughter Annual Summary, 51,662 buffalo were slaughtered nationwide for meat in 2014.

The American Prairie Reserve in Montana is an example of the

Buffalo Commons in action. It's a private organization that formed in 2001 and aims to be the largest wildlife reserve in the contiguous U.S. Its goal is to secure 3.5 million acres of public and private land, which would make the reserve a third larger than Yellowstone National Park. (Remarkably, the reserve, as of 2014, has already secured 305,000 acres of public and private land, where it has already reintroduced buffalo.)

Part of the problem with the plains ecological crisis is a problem of recreation. If you look at a map that shows all the national parks, wilderness areas, and public lands in the country, the plains are practically empty. The United States is 35 percent publicly owned, yet from North Dakota down to Texas only 2.8 percent of the land is. (Kansas is the least publicly owned state, with just 0.92 percent of its land owned by the government.) Because of the lack of public space, there's simply nowhere for travelers to experience and therefore appreciate and wish to take care of the plains. We call them the "flyover" states for good reason: There's really no way to see them other than to fly over or drive through them. Consequently, there's little public pushback to preserve our grasslands and the species that dwell on them. (On the plains, only 1 percent of the native prairie has long-term protection.) That's why Steve Myers, a schoolteacher from Longmont, Colorado, and his idea to create a 1,700-mile Great Plains Trail are so intriguing. The Great Plains Trail, which he aims to finish mapping out by 2018, will closely parallel my route from Montana to Texas and rely on public grasslands and rarely traveled country roads.

Other, more radical, ideas exist, such as returning the plains to its Pleistocene form by reintroducing the megafauna that went extinct around the same time that human settlers arrived from Asia more than 10,000 years ago. It's argued that the plains can't be brought back to their true form without at least 70 percent of the megafauna that abruptly vanished. The camel, which would be reintroduced, is actually a North American animal that migrated to Eurasia and populated the Old World. Coming to America would be a homecoming of sorts. Asian elephants would replace the mammoth and the African lion would replace the North American lions. The elephants and camels, supposedly, would control the encroachment of woody and shrub plants, as they did historically.

It's futile to predict the future because we're all so bad at it, but it was clear to me that the plains' destructive agricultural experiment will continue for the foreseeable future—with bigger and bigger farms, more effective farming technologies, and heaps of taxpayer cash— until the water and oil get too expensive.

I was in southern Kansas walking down a country road when I spotted a big black dog dashing toward me. It hugged the property owner's fence line, keeping its body low to the ground while keeping its wolf eyes trained on me and moving with the sleek-bodied stealth and confidence of a hungry lioness. It was the size of a German shepherd, and had a shiny jet-black coat.

As soon as it got to the gravel road, it took off on a full sprint, snarling through its white fangs. It stopped just feet from me, then lunged at my ankles. I thrust both my trekking poles toward its face. It backed off but continued to closely follow me as I sped forward, separated only by the short length of my trekking poles that I kept pointed at its face.

This wasn't the first time I'd had to deal with crazy country dogs in Kansas. Most times, I'd just ignore them and keep walking. They'd prowl behind me for a bit until they got too far from home, and I'd haughtily refuse to even look their way, a tactic that proved to be fairly effective. Sometimes, when I could tell the dog was merely bluffing— and these dogs were always easy enough to identify—I'd baby-talk it out of its rabid fervor and have the animal nuzzling its head against my thigh in no time.

But this dog, I knew instantly, wasn't the sort that could be wooed. It was savage and bloodthirsty, probably bearing a ferocious love for its family and a dim-witted hatred for everyone else.

It followed me for several minutes, gnashing its teeth and sprinting at me whenever I turned my back to it. My only thought was to keep moving and not let it get in front of me. I used my trekking poles to keep it from biting my legs, but I felt my jackknife glowing in the right pocket of my pants. I knew if it bit me that I'd let it have my arm or leg while I aimed a fatal pierce into its chest or neck.

"Pedro! Pedro!" a little boy cried from the front porch of the home the dog had run from.

Hearing the little boy's calls seemed to incense the dog even more. Pedro followed me for a fifth of a mile and didn't turn back until the man of the house came out and screamed for the dog to return.

Once I was a good distance from the house, I put my pack down and retrieved the canister of bear spray, which I'd mostly forgotten about. Thereafter, on country roads, I'd keep my bear spray strapped to my backpack's chest buckle, ready to be grabbed and discharged within seconds. Between Pedro and the other snarling dogs, I was getting nervous whenever I approached houses on rural roads. I had no choice but to eye all homes—and all dogs—with fear and suspicion.

.   .   .

made it into the tiny town of Potwin, Kansas, on Christmas Eve. I asked a woman if she knew any of the pastors in town. She said she did but that he wouldn't be around until the evening service that night. She invited me into her home, where she fed me chili and cookies. I attended services with her family, took Communion, and slept on the floor of the church balcony.

On Christmas, I continued south to the medium-size city of Augusta (pop. 9,274). It was twenty degrees Fahrenheit outside with blistering twenty-five-mile-per-hour winds. My map said the country road I walked along would lead me over a creek, but when I reached it, I saw that the creek was wide, deep, and frozen, and that there was no bridge. I heaved a large dead branch into the air, and when it fell on the ice, I was encouraged when the creek maintained its solid form. I began to cross it, but after two steps, fault lines spread across the ice under the weight of my foot like cracks in a broken mirror. I quickly turned back to shore, where I began a long detour to another road to find a way across. When I hopped over a tall barbed-wire fence, my maps fell out of my back pocket and were carried away in the brisk wind like fall leaves destined to decompose under a foreign, faraway tree trunk. It was yet another exhausting day, but I'd long ago become as numb to exhaustion as my hands were to the biting cold.

I walked straight east along a road, took a southeasterly shortcut over a cow pasture, then headed south along a new gravel road. On the road, two dogs rocketed out from beneath their porch and charged after me. Their barks were terrifying at first, but once I sized them up—a small white Chihuahua and a young black Lab—I knew I had nothing to worry about.

The Lab kept running after me, but once I parried its barks with baby talk, he let out a relieved whimper and ran up to my legs. He put his two front paws on my hip, I petted his head, and he let out a deep guttural moan, as if I were finally giving him some long-withheld pleasure. I sat down to have a snack and fed him a slice of buffalo jerky.

The dog began to follow me, and I welcomed the company for the first few minutes, but when I realized he wasn't going to stop, I began to yell at him to go home, even threatening him with my sticks when he wouldn't listen. I resolved not to look at or talk to him except to angrily yell at him to go back home. But each time I yelled, the dog would only tuck his tail between his legs and fall on his back submissively.

I secretly adored the dog and had already thought up a name for it (Kansas), but I dared not utter it aloud for fear that—by giving it a name—I would allow this icy acquaintanceship to evolve into something more.

Despite my fantasies, I quickly determined that Kansas was not the best companion for a long walk across Oklahoma and Texas. He was too small and too timid to be able to defend himself against the big angry dogs I was constantly encountering. And he was stupidly fearless around cars and roads, crossing the roadways at whim.

I did well to maintain my vow of silence, but when we reached a busy bridge with narrow shoulders, I knew that Kansas would follow me over the bridge and would very likely get run over. I had to do something.

I made a leash with a thin orange tent guyline, tied it snugly around Kansas's neck, and began walking toward the bridge. Kansas was confused and hesitant, not because he was stubborn but because he clearly had never had a leash put around his neck before.

"Let's practice a bit first," I said.

We got off the bridge and walked back and forth along the grassy shoulder of the road. He got the hang of it, I rewarded him with fond pats on the head, and we successfully crossed. After that, I was determined to train him not to go anywhere near the road, casting discouraging invectives at him when he went to cross but lavishing him with warmth when he hung by my side. By the end of the day, I wondered if he might make a good companion after all. He wasn't the smartest dog in the world, but he clearly had a functional set of legs and a bit of perseverance, which was about as much as I could say for myself. I took him to the Augusta police station, where I explained who I was, what I was doing, as well as the whole dog situation.

They told me they were going to take him to the pound, where he'd remain for three days until the owners claimed him. If no one claimed him, they said they'd have to put him down.

"Put him down?" I said.

Another cop showed up. He put a leash around the dog's neck and tried to pull him into the backseat of his patrol car. Kansas wouldn't budge, so the cop asked me for help. I grabbed his body and struggled to shove Kansas and his flailing limbs into the back. The cop closed the door, and Kansas peered longingly at me through the window.

The cop called churches for me—to see if any would lend me a floor for the night—but there were no offers. The cop then offered to buy me a motel room, but, too prideful to accept money, I declined even though I badly wanted a warm place to stay on so cold a night. I walked downtown to the local movie theater, where they were showing *The Hobbit* in 3-D. It was freezing outside, and the theater had yet to open, so I went into a gas station, where I hoped to buy some coffee and stay warm in a booth for an hour or so. The owner approached me as I drank my cappuccino in the corner of the store and told me I had to leave.

I walked to the movie theater and knocked on the door, hoping someone would let me in. The owner inside, preparing for the movie, said that she was all alone and that I couldn't come in.

I felt pitiful standing out in the cold with the wind blasting in my face on this dark lonely street with no place to go on Christmas. There was irony here—being scorned on a religious holiday and all—but on this trip I had received such generous treatment from so many people that it was impossible for me to feel upset or frustrated. It was as if I had a stockpile of goodness in me, so any sort of injustice or cool treatment had little effect, as I always had fresh memories of kindness.

Eventually the theater opened and I watched *The Hobbit*. I got more than my eight dollars' worth, but I wondered if the film could have benefited from more darkness, more humanity, more reality. Where were the moments of crippling fear? The raw emotion? The knee-buckling pain? Where was the traveler's grime or the hiker's hobble? The shin splints and blisters?

The owner of the theater, who'd been initially leery of me, was so worried about my camping out in the cold that—during the movie—she called the police station and urged them to let me sleep at the station, which I ended up doing.

In the morning, I packed my things and got ready for my day's walk south, but I was held back. Just as the lady in the theater knew she couldn't let me sleep out in the cold, I knew that I couldn't let the dog die in the pound. I decided to wait in town the three days so I could adopt it and take it along with me, but first I had to see if I could contact the dog's owners. I showed the police where the dog had come from on my map, but they said they didn't know how to get the phone number. I decided to put my Internet stalking skills to good use, and I eventually found the phone number of a neighbor of the dog's owner and explained the situation.

Later, I got a call from the owner. "Thank you so much for taking care of our dog," she said. "A dog of ours died last year and many tears were shed. We'll be very happy to have him back."

With that, I threw on my pack and headed south to Oklahoma.

17.

The Night Walker

January 5, 2013

←→

I crossed the Kansas-Oklahoma border and hiked south down the wide grassy shoulder of Highway 77. I walked past Native American casinos and small derelict hovels, as well as a few quaint country homes. Unlike most of the roadways I'd walked so far, the grass along Highway 77 was covered with an appalling amount of litter—flattened cans of Bud Light and Keystone, empty bottles of malt liquor, a tattered white McDonald's bag, a needle, a snowstorm of crushed Styrofoam.

Because nearly every house had a dog, I grew nervous every time I approached one. And because this route through Oklahoma was much more populous than the other places I'd walked through, I spent practically every moment of my day in a state of fear, or in the anticipation of fear, which is pretty much the same thing. Most dogs would turn out to be sweethearts, but many were quite evil and were often from aggressive breeds that had been ill-treated all their lives.

With the hope of walking past homes unnoticed, I took several precautions: I moved to the other side of the road; I stopped whistling, singing, and talking to myself; I placed my feet on asphalt (rather than crispy leaves); and I ceased using my trekking poles—all in order to make as little noise as necessary.

There's no way anyone's living in there, I thought to myself while passing what looked like a junkyard of RVs cluttered around a double-wide with a sagging roof. Just in case somebody was (and just in case there were dogs), I moved to the other side of the highway. Sure enough, a three-legged mongrel that had caught my scent came hobbling out of the scrap heap, barking at me, snarling for a bony ankle. I escaped the mongrel, but now two pit bulls from my side of the road came running at me. I quickly scanned for traffic and scampered across the busy 77 back to the mongrel that I feared less. The pit bulls—quite prudently—decided not to cross, and the mongrel luckily had already limped back to its hovel.

This was how I spent nearly every day in Oklahoma.

I was headed to the Pipeline Crossroads of the World: Cushing, Oklahoma. Cushing is the southern terminus of the 2010 Keystone Pipeline. If the Keystone XL is approved, oil will be piped by a shorter route from Hardisty, Alberta, to Cushing. A second part of the Keystone XL would be built from Cushing to the Gulf Coast refineries in Texas.

I'd been paralleling the pipeline by walking on roads for the past two hundred miles, only occasionally walking the pipe's actual path. Because the pipeline for these last several hundred miles had been straight north to south, it made sense to follow the nearest road, which also heads north to south. But in Oklahoma, the pipeline takes yet another southeasterly turn, so I would have to begin jumping fences again.

The romantic part of me looked forward to new adventures and glorious sights over rarely walked lands: Oklahoma sunsets, rolling green fields, forests of slender pines. But the scaredy-cat in me resented having to once again walk through terrifying cow herds and keep an eye out for zealous landowners.

The state of Oklahoma, which produces the fifth-most oil, has a motley of pipelines, pump jacks, refineries, and tank farms. I hadn't seen so many pipeline markers since Alberta.

All day, semis zoomed past me, each hauling three giant thirty-six-inch-diameter Keystone XL pipes in the shape of giant cigarettes that would be buried in Oklahoma and Texas soil. (The southern portion of Keystone XL—from Cushing to Port Arthur—had recently received presidential support and was being laid.) It was demoralizing to have to watch all these trucks, all these pipes, and all this giant equipment being transported. It made me feel small and powerless and hopeless. Half the XL was already being put into the ground. Why bother fighting something that's pretty much inevitable? Why bother even caring? We're warned constantly that there could be a tipping point right around the corner, where climate change could begin to speed up exponentially. In many areas of the world, it already has.

How much time do we have? Bill McKibben, in his *Rolling Stone* essay "Global Warming's Terrifying New Math," claims we shouldn't raise the temperature more than two degrees Celsius for fear that droughts, floods, and storms could shake the foundation of our civilization. "[Two degrees Celsius has] become the bottomest of bottom lines," says McKibben. (As of 2012, we'd already raised it 0.8 degrees

Celsius.) On a gloomier note, he adds, "Before we knew those numbers, our fate had been likely. Now, barring some massive interven-
tion, it seems certain."

Retired NASA scientist James Hansen says that if the Keystone
XL is approved and the tar sands expand "it will be game over for the
climate." Even E. O. Wilson, who usually comes across as more hopeful than other environmentalists, concedes that the conservation ethic
"has generally come too late . . . to save the most vulnerable of life
forms."

When I think about our culture's addiction to fossil fuel, its indifference to the natural world, and the sheer impossibility of any major
change happening soon, I can't help but despair. Almost as depressing
as an inevitable collapse is how powerless I feel as an individual. A
life-ending meteor hurtling toward us is one thing. In that case, none
of us can really do anything, so we might as well buy a twelve-pack,
throw a few steaks on the grill, and enjoy the show. But climate change
is different. It appears we *can* do something about it. But change is
only possible if it's a collective "we" rather than a lonely "I." So where
does that leave those individuals who care deeply about the planet but
are no more than a scattered minority?

Our national myths do not help us deal with the anxieties of climate change. Our "superhero" culture wants us to take matters into
our own hands, stand up for what's right, take the leap when we reach
the edge of a rooftop, and never back down even in the face of impossible odds. We're at the point when we're supposed to act, but signing
another online petition, changing to a more efficient lightbulb, and
joining a march doesn't feel like enough.

Wendell Berry says, "The line ought to be drawn without fail
wherever it can be drawn easily." Berry was talking less about climate

change and more about managing our consumption, but the message still applies: We should make sacrifices when they're easy to make. This is enough for me on most days. But there are other days when I worry if my commitment to environmentalism is too weak and if I'm squandering a life that could be spent doing something truly valuable. But what is valuable action? Environmental terrorism has a romantic appeal, but I'm not convinced that destruction is an effective way to build a movement, and I'm not at all eager to spend a life term in federal prison. Maybe the best advice comes from Reinhold Niebuhr, who wrote what has become known as the Serenity Prayer.

> God, grant me the serenity
> to accept the things I cannot change;
> the courage to change the things I can;
> and the wisdom to know the difference.

Paul Kingsnorth, an environmental activist in the U.K., is one of first to come clean about his despair over climate change and what he sees as inevitable doom. Some consider the despair movement as a way of giving up or abandoning one's moral duty. But Kingsnorth, a founder of the Dark Mountain Project, which is a network, its web site describes, "of writers, artists and thinkers who have stopped believing the stories our civilization tells itself," argues that we should be honest with ourselves. Dougald Hine, a cofounder of the group, says, "Let's not pretend we're not feeling despair. Let's sit with it for a while. Let's be honest with ourselves and with each other. And then as our eyes adjust to the darkness, what do we start to notice?"

Despair, I've found, is a seductive alternative to a life of civic participation. Despair absolves us of responsibility. It's a way of managing guilt: If the world's going to hell in a handbasket, we might as well jack up the thermostat and live it up. *If our efforts are futile, then there's nothing to feel guilty about, right?* There's a "comfort in clarity" in accepting that doom is certain. If we have a clear vision of the future, at least we know our relation to it. If we leave no chance for success, fortune, or surprise, then with our knowledge of doom, we can live with a semblance of order, logic, and predictability even in a soon-to-be-apocalyptic world. Strangely, there's comfort here.

One wonders if our leading public environmentalists are talking about climate change with their followers in a destructive way. It seems as if it's their aim to scare the living shit out of us by offering doomsday prophecies of a soon-to-be-uninhabitable Earth and interpreting every nasty storm as a harbinger of the apocalypse. Fear can provoke action; it can get us to care. But how long can we live in a state of anxiety before burning out and resorting to despair? Scientists like Hansen and McKibben have every right to scare us, and their methods are no doubt scientifically sound, but one can't help but wonder if the end-of-the-world rhetoric is a wise policy for sustaining a movement.

In Ponca City, a man in a big cowboy hat yelled at me from his red car as I crossed an intersection. His name was Everett and he offered to buy me a sandwich. I ordered a Big Mac and fries at the local McDonald's. Everett was a retired construction worker and a recovering alcoholic.

"Has alcohol been a problem you've had to deal with for a long time?" I asked.

"Not since I quit," Everett said.

He asked me why I was doing this and I explained to him that I wanted to learn about the XL and also live an adventurous life.

"Are you a Christian?" he asked.

"No, I'm afraid not," I said.

"Well, you have a light in you," he said. "I can see it."

"I don't know about that, Everett," I said. "But thanks."

"I can see it," he said.

In Morrison, I set up my tent in the dugout of a baseball field so I could have a little more protection from the rain. The next day—New Year's Eve—the rain continued, so I decided to spend the day snacking at the local gas station and the night back in the dugout. An oil-man named Dusty spotted me sitting in the gas-station booth and asked if I'd like to spend New Year's Eve with his family.

Wayne, a former police officer in the town of Ripley, offered me a night in a trailer that he was renovating. On the road the next day, he pulled over and handed me a bottle of orange juice and some warm biscuits and gravy.

I'd tried trespassing over fields and pastures along the pipeline path, but I quickly determined that it was too dangerous; it led me too close to people's homes. I felt as if I were constantly being watched. Oklahoma is nothing like Alberta, where one family takes care of ten thousand acres and where I might see only one home over the course of the day. Here, the pipe's path took me past many small impoverished homes. Dogs heard my footsteps and howled. I could see their thick white bodies moving behind stands of trees. I kept my bear spray, with the cap off, in the side pocket of my pants, prepared to douse any growling curs with a mouthful of cayenne.

This was poor country. Lawns were covered with rusty swing sets, rickety trampolines, faded multicolored plastic tricycles. To the side of each home was a junkyard of useless vehicles. Dogs lived miserable lives on short chains. Garbage was everywhere.

I felt pity but also a sense of disgust: pity for the miserable living conditions and disgust for the cultural poverty that was as much choice as affliction. It's easy to blame the travails of the poor on whatever political party you most dislike. These parties probably deserve part of the blame, but one can't help but think critically of these lifestyles when hardships are partially self-inflicted. The garbage, the obesity, the drug addictions, the alcoholism, the glowing television sets in living rooms, the obsession with huge fuel-inefficient pickup trucks.

Part of this, no doubt, has to do with growing up in an area where one doesn't have many opportunities and where social mobility is stunted. Yet I could see that this poverty also derived from an almost-flagrant isolationism, an extreme sense of privacy, a self-expulsion from society. Nearly every home had a fence around it and a snarling cur under the porch. There were countless signs reading BEWARE OF DOG, PRIVATE PROPERTY, and NO TRESPASSING. I presumed that it was just as unlikely for a neighbor to knock on one of these front doors as it was for an outsider. How could there be any sense of community when neighbors couldn't visit one another? How could we understand the world when we're secluded and holed up in hovels? And just as their homes are closed off to the outside world, so are many of their minds. I tried speaking with one man about climate change, and all he said was "Well, did you get that information from the liberal or the Democrat scientists? I tell you, there ain't no way I'm voting for someone who wants to make my gas more expensive." It was moments like these when I'd lose all hope for meaningful action on climate change.

After a few close calls with dogs, I decided to stick with highways, which would add many miles to my trip, but I figured it would be better than walking in constant fear.

Because Cushing is one of the oil hubs of the world, I expected the city to be an island of prosperity in a sea of poverty. But I quickly learned that Cushing was anything but. Grass was taking over the sidewalks. Brick buildings were crumbling. Families lived in aged trailers alongside packs of wild dogs locked inside tiny fenced enclosures. We're told that pipelines bring wealth and jobs to communities along their paths, yet there in Cushing—at the center of the oil universe—it was hard to tell if you were still in a First World country.

I walked through Cushing as quickly as I could and felt the terrible desire, for the first time in my journey, to reach the end.

I made it into Atoka, Oklahoma, just before nightfall. It was now my standard procedure to go straight to churches to seek advice about where I should set up my tent. Most times they'd let me camp on their lawns, and sometimes they'd let me sleep on the floor inside. I spoke with the youth minister of a Baptist church, who very kindly directed me to the backyard of a vacant lot in town owned by a relative.

The town of Atoka, the minister told me, suffers from some of the typical maladies of poverty: theft, drug abuse, broken families. "A quarter of the town is beneath the poverty line," he said.

He drew for me a map of the town with directions to the vacant lot. It was getting dark when I set out, and I took a wrong turn, which led me down a street very clearly suffering from poverty, where a rottweiler, attached to a leash that looked about as brittle as one of my

beard hairs, lunged at me over and over again. I kept walking, thinking I knew where I was, until the road ended. To my side, I saw three
men in the dark standing idly against the side of a home. I didn't have
any reason to think they had anything malicious in mind, but I was
scared nevertheless.

I called the minister on my phone, and he drove out and rode
alongside me as he guided me to his aunt's lot. While the vacant lot
was still in a poor part of town, he said it was safe, and it appeared to
be so. The property was bordered with trees, so if I set up my tent
behind the lot's empty house that was propped up on concrete blocks,
no one would be able to spot me.

I set up my tent and inside I ate cans of tuna and sardines (that
the youth minister's wife had given me) for dinner and finished reading *The Lord of the Rings*. I settled into a deep, peaceful sleep as I did
most every night.

I woke up a couple of hours later to the sound of a dog sniffing my
tent. Curious to see what breed it was, I sat up and looked out one of
my tent's portholes. It wasn't to the right of me, so I looked out the
left porthole.

It was two thirty a.m., and that's when I saw a man walking toward my tent. He was coming straight for me. He had the gait of a
horror movie villain: a springy yet hobbled lurch, confident and steady.
It was dark, but I could see that he was carrying something big, some
large hand tool or weapon perhaps.

I was completely paralyzed by fear. I could have started to prepare myself for the attack. I could have opened my jackknife, taken
off the cap of my bear spray, or simply dialed 911, but I did nothing. I
could hardly even breathe. I'd always imagined myself doing some-

thing Bruce Willis–esque in moments like this, but instead I simply watched him walk toward me, and all he had to do was unzip my tent and clunk me over the head with whatever he was carrying.

But he continued past my tent into the woods, his dog following at his heels.

What should I do? Perhaps he was harmless, but now maybe he's thinking to himself that he has an easy target? Maybe he'll come back with more people? Why did he walk within just a few feet of my tent? Feeling more vulnerable than ever, I called the cops.

"This isn't quite an emergency," I said nervously over the phone. "But I'm walking across the continent and I'm camping in Atoka in a tent behind an abandoned house in a vacant lot on X Street." It wasn't until I said this to the operator that I realized just how crazy what I was doing was. "I don't know, maybe you could have a patrol car come out?"

Ten minutes later, two police cars came by. I emerged from my tent and the cops, who'd walked into the backyard, pointed their bright flashlights into my squinting eyes. I explained what had happened, and they seemed pretty nonchalant about it.

"He was probably just coming out to get a look at ya," said one officer, as if approaching a random tent in the middle of the night with a medieval weapon were as normal a thing to do as taking out the trash.

"Yeah, he was probably coming out to get a look at ya," said the other.

I was grateful that the cops came out, yet I wasn't at all put at ease. I lay in my sleeping bag for the rest of the night, waking to any noise, gripping my weapons in each hand.

. . .

I n the morning, I headed east along Highway 3.

That night, I slept in the town of Lane next to a convenience store, where I used the Wi-Fi to begin the second season of *Downton Abbey*. The next day, I walked toward Antlers. I knew from the forecast that I was going to get hit hard by rain, so I made sure to tightly seal all of my stuff in waterproof garbage bags inside my backpack.

And sure enough, the storm came. There was booming thunder and white-hot flashes of lightning. There was nowhere to take cover, so I kept walking on the grassy shoulder of the highway. The rain picked up: Thousands of big lumpy raindrops hit me at once like alien missiles. Even with my rain gear on, the rain managed to seep through all my clothing, saturating everything. It was the heaviest rain I'd ever seen, let alone walked in. My hands, wound tightly around my trekking poles, no longer had much feeling, and I could feel my body fighting to keep me warm. "KEEP WALKING!" I screamed into the storm. "C'MON!"

At one point, the rain was coming down so hard I thought it might knock me over. It was a biblical storm: equal parts wicked and cleansing. In a matter of twenty minutes, three cars pulled over to ask if I needed a ride, and each time I had to explain that I was on a walking expedition.

I longed for shelter. *Where will I sleep tonight?* I imagined a lonely middle-aged widow—a rancher's wife with straw-colored hair— calling me from the porch of her home to come inside for shelter. "What are you doing out there?" she'd yell. "Get yourself in here!" At first, she'd think I was a homeless person, and I'd come in, and she'd say, "For heaven's sake, you must be freezing. Let's get you out of those wet clothes." I'd go into the bathroom, and through the gap between the door and the wall, she'd catch sight of me peeling off my shirt, noticing, to her astonishment, that I had neither the withered limbs nor the lumpy gut of a bum but the finely chiseled physique of a hiker. "Dear God," she'd mutter to herself involuntarily, suddenly flooded with desires that had long lain comatose in her grieving heart.

Having received no such invitation, when—freezing, saturated, and exhausted—I got to Antlers (which boasts of being the Deer Capital of the World), I went straight to the local pizzeria and changed into my dry clothes in the bathroom before ordering myself a supreme pizza. A family with two little girls, who'd seen me come in, was curious about what I was doing in Antlers so they came over and asked. I told them tales of charging moose, stampeding cows, and crazy Nebraskan cops. I left out the dilapidated homes, crazy dogs, and strange men walking toward me at night, thinking that I had a good reason to remember the better side of Oklahoma. The girls posed for pictures with me, saying they were going to talk about my trip with their class, and the grandfather left ten dollars on the table, went to the register, and paid for my pizza.

18.

The Preacher

February 2, 2013

← →

I was sitting on an olive-colored couch surrounded by three preachers in the lobby of an extravagantly furnished Baptist church.

I'd come to the church, as I often did, to ask for a patch of grass to set up my tent. The youth minister I first spoke with said I could and that I should feel free to charge my electronics in the lobby until they had to lock down the church after their Wednesday night service. He asked why I was hiking the pipeline. I sensed that he was one of those open-minded, progressive-thinking churchmen, so I said, "Well, I guess I'm one of those whacko environmentalists."

Noting that we were in conservative oil country, he said, "Just don't tell our church members that. Say you're just going on a walk or something."

His partner, Pastor James—a middle-aged, lean-bodied preacher looking dapper in his pastel pink dress shirt, tie, and trousers—came up to me, introduced himself, and asked, "Has anyone on your journey talked to you about Jesus?"

"Of course," I said, surprised with how fluidly the lie had exited my mouth.

While I'd interacted with countless preachers and Christian practitioners over the past five months, no one up until this point had attempted to indoctrinate me. In my life before the trip, though, I'd been preached to many times, and because I did not want to be preached to again, I thought I'd try to outmaneuver the pastor and dodge having to listen to what would most certainly be an agonizing monologue. But when he asked, "What do you think it takes to get into heaven?" I knew there was no way out.

"Well, I don't have a denomination," I said. "But I believe in the church of caring for our fellow man and Mother Earth."

"But have you accepted Jesus as your personal savior?" he asked.

"No, but I have a Gideon Bible," I said, pulling out the tiny Bible given to me in Kansas, as if it were a magical amulet that would stun him into silence.

"And have you read it?" he asked.

"No," I said, feeling the snare tighten around my ankle. "But my mother's Catholic. And I was baptized Catholic."

"But you don't go to church?"

"No . . . I guess I don't."

Pastor James stared more than he looked. He pointed his gaze toward my eyes but not into them. He was more machine than man, more dry doctrine than deliberate thought, more steel than soul. He had the sort of half-dead stare of someone who's gone through some horrible experience that had taken his humanity.

"Hasn't read the Bible. Doesn't go to church," he muttered, listing my sins. His suspicions confirmed, he was clearly becoming excited. He leaned his head back, puffed out his chest, and rubbed his chin with two fingers before explaining that we're all sinners, that Jesus died for our sins, and that I needed to accept Jesus as my personal savior to get into heaven.

I was slightly embarrassed for him. Two other preachers were standing around me, and I thought they might be thinking, *Oh boy, here goes crazy Pastor James again.* But I could see that they—nodding their heads in assent and chiming in with amens—were getting just as much enjoyment out of this as Pastor James was.

The whole idea of someone "dying for my sins" did absolutely nothing for me. If I killed or stole or did something undeniably bad, what difference would it make if someone else died for those sins? How does dying for my sins and my future sins make my sins any more forgivable? Why does this crazy story work for so many people!? And what's with this obsession with sinning? The more I thought about it, the more I realized that I don't really sin. I drink to be merry, I lie for the sake of social harmony, and I lust because I'm stuck with a twenty-nine-year-old-guy's body. I don't feel guilty for any of the above, as they aren't wrong, and when I do something wrong, my conscience catches it and I do my best to not do it again.

I didn't get the sense that Pastor James was preaching to me out of a sense of compassion or that he truly cared about the fate of my soul. Rather, converting me was only a sort of game for him to play. As I sat on his couch in his church in my dusty clothes, he did not see me as his equal but as someone he could wield power over. I was little more than sport to him.

I sat there quietly, politely listening while thinking to myself, *I'm smarter than all you fools.* I knew that Pastor James, so blinded by his faith, would never have an intellectual discussion for the rest of his life. I was tired of being lectured to by zealots and global-warming deniers.

I was, of course, quite touched by the help I'd received from Christians along my path. And I found that almost all of them were moved to help not because they wished to convert me but because they found joy in helping. I was once a person who would scoff at the idea of becoming Christian, and while I knew I'd never become a true believer, I'd started to think it might be possible one day—if I ever settled down—to join a progressive, tolerant, we-interpret-the-Bible-metaphorically church if only to become part of a community and heighten my sense of charity.

"Well, I have lots of time to think on my walk," I said to Pastor James, hoping that that would end the conversation, as he could then rest assured that he'd planted a seed of thought in my head and that I'd be mulling over his words of wisdom on my long walk. But all he heard was "I have lots of time."

"But you don't have lots of time!" he said. "None of us know God's plan!" The service was about to start, so he plucked a pamphlet from a shelf titled, "Do you know for certain that you have ETER-NAL LIFE?" and handed it to me with a look on his face that seemed to say, *If I didn't get through to him, this will.*

'd begun to feel a little wimpy.

In Oklahoma, because I'd been so terrified of everything—and because I felt like I'd used up eight of my lives on this trip—I decided I ought to be extra careful with my final ninth. So, instead of walking along the pipe in Texas (which was being laid by pipeline crews), I decided to walk on the shoulders of major highways where I wouldn't get in trouble.

But the walk had become fairly boring. There was less interaction out on the highway, less adventure, and certainly less Keystone XL. I'd already walked many miles across the state without having had a meaningful conversation with a landowner affected by the XL. I felt like I was cutting a corner.

But after I received an e-mail from a guy named Storms Reback, who asked if he could join me, I thought having a partner in crime would make me feel more comfortable about following the pipe closely again. I also received a Facebook message from a young lady who was a PhD student at a university in Texas, who wondered if she could meet up with me, too.

Storms is a lean and affable and witty forty-two-year-old writer from Austin, Texas, where he lives with his wife and child. He's the author of three books about poker; his latest is called *Ship It Holla Ballas!*, about a group of teenagers who made millions of dollars playing online poker before it was outlawed. It had sold well and the movie rights had been purchased, but Storms had had enough of writing about poker so, feeling the same strange draw to the Keystone XL I'd felt, he decided to join me for a week or so.

He met me in the small town of Arp, Texas, where I had a package to pick up. We hit it off right away, as if we'd been friends in a previous life, talking about books, hiking, and the state of the environment.

I asked a man at the post office where I might be able to set up my tent in town, and he told me I could set it up on his front lawn. Once we got talking, and once he noticed I was very much in need of a shower (which he later confided to me), he offered his guest house, where Storms would meet me. The next day, Storms and I took off south. I was a third of the way through Texas, with about two hundred miles to go to Port Arthur.

Storms and I, after heading south out of Arp, quickly came to the pipeline path, which was essentially a one-hundred-foot-wide dirt road. Here, one of the many pipeline-laying companies had removed the trees and grass to make way for the business of laying the pipe. We walked next to a deep ten-foot trench into which the pipes would be laid. The pipes, off to the side, were all propped up on pallets so that cranes could pick them up and set them in the trench. Colorful flags were festooned over the width of the path.

Storms was eager to jump into this adventure. "Well, what do you think?" he said, excited, looking down the forbidden dirt path.

"I say we go for it," I said.

And so we set off over the dirt path, which was a fine hiking trail except for the barbed-wire fences every hundred yards or so. After nearly forty minutes of easy walking, we heard a truck rumbling behind us. It pulled up and two Smith County cops came out.

"We probably shouldn't be on here, should we?" I said.

"No, you shouldn't," said one of the cops.

Our licenses were taken and the policewoman explained to us that there'd been protesters from the Tar Sands Blockade in the area in the past, so the landowners who'd caught sight of us thought we might be them. Eventually, they let us go, and we promised we'd stick to county roads closest to the pipe.

We dealt with the typical travails of walking across the occasionally impoverished Heartland, but now that I had a partner, the dogs were less vicious, less ambitious, less confident. And I noticed that I no longer was walking through Texas with fear. The presence of another human being had magically put me at ease.

Jessica and her dog, Benny, met up with us in the tiny ghost town of Consort, Texas, which has not only a church and an empty volunteer fire department but also an ideal camping setup at the pastor's house: a fire pit, a big lawn to set up tents, and church bathrooms.

Jessica was tall, fit, had long brown hair tied up in a ponytail, and wore hip hiker's garb. Storms took off to bed early, leaving Jessica and me alone by the fire with a bottle of whiskey. I watched the light of the fire dance over her cheekbones and began to appreciate that I was in the presence of a Smart and Attractive Woman. I went to the bathroom, worried I was going to throw up (she and I had finished the whole bottle), but fortune took pity on me and the urge passed. When I careened back to the fire, the coals had mellowed and Jessica was sitting on the pit's rim. I sat next to her. She was talking about something, and I felt this terrible, awful desire to simply rest my tired, vulnerable, needy head on her shoulder. It had been more than half a year since I'd touched another human being. The alcohol had duly drowned my inhibitions, so I went for it, and she let out an *awww* and gushed out words of pent-up fondness. "You're so nice," she said. "And I really love what you're doing on this trip. I'm going to take you back to my tent and I'm going to snuggle you the whole night." I poured water over the fire and got in her tent, where I lay with her the rest of the night next to her dog, who didn't seem at all fazed by the presence of this intruding gentleman caller. If there's anything more revitalizing to a guy than lying with a beautiful woman, I've yet to find it.

In the morning, Storms caught sight of me leaving Jessica's tent (which made me feel like a rock star) with what he later described as a "sheepish grin." I said good-bye to Jessica, and my grin went away when I was hit by the full force of the hangover. An hour into our day's walk, I had to lie down in a bed of pine needles and sleep off my sickness on the shoulder of the road for two hours while Storms read on his iPad. I took a bite out of a granola bar, said I was going to throw up, slept for an hour more, and woke up feeling like a new man, telling Storms that I was "all the way back."

We walked through East Texas pine country, sometimes on dirt roads completely shrouded in the shadows of the pines' long bushy limbs. The homes in this hilly country looked like battered schooners riding on ocean waves.

Mike Bishop is a former Marine, a Vietnam vet, a retired chemist, and, at the age of sixty-four, a first-year med student. We met him at a café in Douglass, and he invited us over for a bonfire at his place.

Bishop had made national headlines the month before when a judge brought the construction of the Keystone XL to a screeching halt. Bishop's contract with TransCanada stated that the company would be transporting crude oil when, in fact, it would be shipping dilbit (short for "diluted bitumen"), a heavier, more corrosive, more toxic substance.

He told us about how the pipe was being laid just one hundred feet from his home, where he took care of his wife, who had Alzheimer's, and his sixteen-year-old daughter. Bishop was fiery, sharp, blunt, and maybe a bit crazy. He spoke nonstop for the next hour.

"I'm sixty-four years old," said Bishop. "My daddy's been dead for many, many years. He taught me three things. He said, 'Mike, people are driven by money, power, sex, or all of the above.' That's it. There is no other motivation in the world. So follow the money. That's the only thing here because TransCanada is not fucking anybody except me and other landowners."

We walked to his house, where Bishop gave us a tour. Next to his white mailbox, overtaken by rust, were two flags: an upside-down American flag and a yellow flag with a serpent that read DON'T TREAD ON ME. His home was a quaint shack, the eaves speckled a moldy green. The composition of his property, apart from the XL's dirt path, was serenely bucolic, with a swath of green grass bordered by pines and a gentle gush of a stream meandering through. It was quiet and misty.

"I told them," Bishop continued, "'I don't like you. I don't like your company. I don't like the fact that you can bully people around. I don't like the fact that you threaten to put me in jail on my own fucking property. But I'll tell you what I'll do. I got another six-acre tract of land. You put your pipeline anywhere on that six acres. Anywhere you want. For free. I don't want your money. I will move any buildings, any fences, anything I've got over there. I will move it for you. Just keep it away from where I raise my children and from where I am now raising my grandchildren.'"

When TransCanada didn't agree to this, Bishop got angry. Yet he didn't get any support from conservatives in the area, who should, at least theoretically, he figured, be in support of private-property rights.

"I don't think the government needs to be telling me what to do in my bedroom with my wife or another man. I don't care if you two go get married or me and him get married," Bishop said, pointing at me. "That's our business. But conservatism has gotten a bad name in the past twenty years, so I said, 'You know what? No more.' For years I thought this climate change was a bunch of crap. Then I started studying it, and said, 'I'm through with the Republican party, I'm through with the bullshit.'

"You don't know how many nights I've laid up here thinking about not killing anybody but shooting them in the butt with a .22. I could conceal in those woods. They would never find me. You don't want to kill nobody, but you hit a guy in the knee or the butt and he's never going to forget what happened. And then the next guy down the line is going to say, 'I don't know if I want to go to work for these people.' And you just go down the line shooting people in the butt. Then, I thought, wait a minute, these are guys trying to feed their families. They're doing the same thing I would do if I were in their shoes. You can't be angry with them. You've got to focus your attention on the company."

Bishop stopped in the middle of his thought to listen to the thrum of croaking frogs.

"Listen to that. Hear that? How long do you think that's going to last when these fucking machines start coming over here?"

In the morning, he awoke early to bring us coffee and wish us a fond farewell.

"Do you have a gun or a knife?" he asked.

"I have a knife and some bear spray," I said.

"Do you have a KA-BAR?"

"I don't think so."

"Are you skilled in martial arts?"

"No, I haven't had to deal with anything like that."

"I am amazed, dude. Let me tell you, I'm a tough guy and I wouldn't be caught dead walking the roads down here anywhere that pipeline is. Those people scare me. Let me tell you something. When I win in the end, they're going to try to kill me."

I may never have been as flattered as when Bishop waved us off and yelled in his Texan drawl: "Let me tell ya. You guys got balls."

. . .

torms and I continued our southward march across Texas. We slept
in an abandoned church parsonage, on church lawns, and when we
couldn't find any churches, we knocked on doors asking for advice
about where to camp, hoping that a homeowner would offer his or
her lawn.

The weather had turned moist and sticky. The pine forest turned
into a viny jungle full of chirping birdsong and the choral hum of in-
sect kingdoms. Salamanders kept warm atop guardrails, and the grassy
roadsides were strewn with the carcasses of wild pigs, rat-tailed opos-
sums, and the brittle shells of armadillos. Turkey vultures, in great
flocks, hovered over the road, seeking their next mangled feast.

We knocked on the door of a small home and asked a guy named
Barney if there was a church nearby. Before we could explain who we
were, what we were doing, and where we were going, he offered us his
guest house.

Barney, a "thirty-three-carat Cajun from Louisiana," as he described himself, is a guitarist in a gospel band who said God gave him
a gift to be able "to play anything with a string." He had stage-three
melanoma. The treatments suppressed his immune system, and we
saw him get sicker as the evening wore on. He said he served in Vietnam, and after he was wounded, he refused to go back. He was thrown
in jail for three months. In Germany, a lieutenant called him a coward.
"You ain't been over there," Barney said to him. "You don't know
what you're talking about, motherfucker."

Barney had some rather progressive views on immigration because he'd raised two Mexican-born boys who were taken away from
him after they'd grown up and were in their forties. But that was the

end of his progressivism. After he'd invited us into his home for milk and chocolate cake, he went on a rant about how the United States was becoming the Soviet Union, calling Nancy Pelosi and Dianne Feinstein "lot lizards" and "road whores," and complaining how it was only a matter of time before we'd become a dictatorial state like all other countries with strong gun-control laws. Having had such conversations with old white guys a hundred times on this trip already, I made an excuse to leave, abandoning poor Storms with Barney.

Barney would tell us later that he was in support of the pipeline. "Anything that can give a man a job is good to me," he said.

Jobs, jobs, JOBS!

This is all I heard wherever I went. Everything that creates jobs must be GOOD!

No one understood that the pipeline wouldn't create that many jobs. For all the miles of laid pipeline that I'd walked over in Canada and Kansas, I didn't see one pipeline worker. And having seen the toll that oil and pipeline jobs have on workers brings into question just how "good" these jobs really are. Although the pipeliners are well paid, they have to live far from their families in motels or trailer parks for months on end. And from what I saw, Fort McMurray, Alberta—where the oilmen of the tar sands live—is no Norman Rockwell painting. Men aren't walking to work in hard hats each morning carrying lunch boxes and coming home to hugs and kisses from their children each night. Most all of the workers in Fort McMurray have left their families, and between the long hours, the morally ambiguous nature of their job, and the utter absence of spirituality and civic engagement in their lives, many turn to alcohol, drugs, gambling, and prostitutes. And it's obvious that many of them aren't putting their hard-earned dollars in cookie jars for rainy days but toward these fleeting enjoyments.

I'd begun to think that a man will not morally object to any job—whether the job requires that he bulldoze forests, make land mines, or poison his neighbor's water—if it means he'll get a paycheck to feed and shelter his family. I say this only partly demoralized. The North American conscience seems designed to very admirably care for self and family, but rare is the person whose conscience is piqued by the sufferings of dwindling species, of a warming planet, or of the fate of generations to come. Unburdened by such abstract thoughts, we wish for little more than a fridge full of food, a big truck, a warm home, and a happy family, and we think it nonsensical—if we think of it at all—to worry about a future we can never really predict and certainly will never see. And while this all seems very shortsighted, it is not without its own logic.

But I never said anything like this to Barney or any of the people I met. They were all older than I was, and because they're old and I was young, they assumed they knew more. And because I spoke little, they thought I knew little. But because they spoke a lot, I knew they didn't know much. Each person spoke to me as if they were doing me some great service, as if they were imparting sage wisdom from ancient texts. But more often than not, I saw that they were propagandized, only regurgitating rumors they'd heard at the local café or half-remembered falsehoods they saw on the TV. They talked in absolutes, spoke expertly on every issue, and rarely if ever would you hear someone say, "Well, I guess I don't know much about that." They weren't free-thinking men, but stone tablets onto which dogma had etched its wicked creed.

When I started this trip, I wondered if I had been living too much in a bubble. Perhaps I'd been reading too many *New York Times* articles. Perhaps I'd put too much faith in peer-reviewed science.

Perhaps—surrounded by open-minded, well-educated, progressives—I was missing the bigger picture. Perhaps if I left academe and went out to the Heartland, I'd tap into the wisdom of the prairie and the farmers who worked it. Maybe they knew the land and skies and environment in ways we suburbanites and city dwellers didn't. Maybe I'd find that they had good reason to deny man-made climate change.

But not one person I encountered had said anything even halfway intelligent when denying global warming. No one had read books or articles on the issue, and they couldn't begin to understand how peer-reviewed science works. They saw themselves as too freewilled and independent to be duped into accepting something that an accomplished and well-trained scientist says is true. But these skeptics are only selectively skeptical. They think themselves enlightened for resisting all this new proof and remaining steadfast in mistrusting anything that someone else says. But it is a false enlightenment to accept only those ideas that align with one's worldview and reject those that don't.

I found myself reading a number of Civil War biographies on this trip. I read Tony Horwitz's *Midnight Rising* about John Brown's raid on Harpers Ferry; Doris Kearns Goodwin's *Team of Rivals* about Lincoln and his cabinet; and Jean Edward Smith's biography of Ulysses S. Grant. It didn't occur to me until then that I might have been drawn to the history of the Civil War because of its similarities with our current climate-change crisis.

Like during the pre–Civil War era, one half of the country is supportive of a cruel and unjust institution—or, to be more specific, a clearly destructive and unsustainable way of life—and the other half (though abolitionists weren't quite half the country) finds something morally reprehensible in our fossil-fuel free-for-alls and their environmental implications. And just as we view the supporters of slavery as backward, simple-minded, and even quaint, future generations may look upon the deniers of today with a similar mix of disbelief, scorn, and amusement.

But perhaps it's not so simple. Most deniers are old, and as one forward-thinking pastor explained to me, people have a hard time believing something they haven't experienced in their lifetime. Lincoln, in one of those moments of great magnanimity that he is known for, said:

> [The Southerners] are just what we would be in their situation. If slavery did not now exist amongst them, they would not introduce it. If it did now exist amongst us, we should not instantly give it up . . . I surely will not blame them for not doing what I should not know how to do myself.

Since they've lived in a world run on coal, gas, and oil that up until recently has caused little perceivable damage, perhaps I should have some level of sympathy for the deniers. As a young person, unsettled in life, it was easy for me to accept the idea of change, even bold change. But for the deniers, their whole lives have been built around the consumption of fossil fuels, and, in a way, it seemed almost natural for them to resist change.

S torms and I made it to the town of Wells. Storms was planning on heading back home to his wife and child in Austin the next day, so he was eager to talk to more landowners who had something to say about the XL since he was thinking about writing an article about it and our hike. Reverend David Goodwin at the Methodist church, who very kindly let us spend the night at his home, told us he knew a guy named Bobby who had a lot to say on the XL and that this guy had special knowledge of XL protesters being paid for their activism.

Reverend David told us about his spinal cord being crushed when his vehicle rolled down a mountainside in Germany while he was serving in the army. He didn't experience any symptoms until two years later when he suddenly could no longer move his left arm. And then everything below his waist stopped working, too. His doctors told him that with his condition (called syringomyelia) he had five years before the rest of his body would quit on him.

He said he was spiritually healed at a retreat six years after the accident. Three years after that, David had an experience with God while he was in meditative prayer.

"I was telling him how beautiful the world he created is," David said. "And God said, 'Raise your left arm,' and I said, 'It don't work.' I just felt this thing saying, 'Raise your left arm.' And I was like, 'It don't work.' He was like, 'Raise your left arm.' And I was like, 'God, it doesn't work. You know it doesn't work. It hasn't worked since 1994.'"

And that's when David's arm shot up in the air.

"I was like, 'What in the world?' I'm freaking out. I'm scared to move my arm because it shot up by itself. I'm scared. I'm looking at it like it's a ghost. I slowly brought it down. I'm in my wheelchair and I'm riding as fast as I can to find somebody to show them that my arm was working. I said, 'I'm going to walk in a year.' So I just went home and I had 120 hours of physical therapy and I started doing everything they told me not to do, and got into a swimming pool and started teaching my body to do what I thought I needed to do. It took almost exactly a year." David had since become a reverend at the church in Wells, where he and his wife have raised two kids.

David drove Storms to Bobby's as I pedaled a bicycle behind their car.

Bobby was a bulky guy, gray haired, and probably in his early fifties. He wore a camo jacket and blue jeans. Reverend David introduced me as a writer gathering stories on the pipeline who's "sort of against it." Bobby, looking at my beard and slightly ragged clothing, saw in me the very protesters who staged demonstrations near his land.

"Now let me ask you this!" he exclaimed, scowling, pointing his finger at my face. "Do you know how much a gallon of gasoline costs in Saudi Arabia?"

"No," I said.

"You don't!" he harrumphed. "That's interesting. Do you know what a liter is?" he asked.

I was tired of avoiding conflict, avoiding the topic of climate change, avoiding speaking my mind to men like Bobby.

Bring it on, bitch! I thought to myself. *I'm taking this conversation all the way to climate change.*

"Yeah, I know what a liter is," I said.

"Well a liter of gasoline in Saudi Arabia costs sixteen cents."

"Yeah, but we won't get the Keystone XL oil," I said, gathering where he was going with his point. "Or at least we won't get all of it. Valero, the refining company, which would get 20 percent of the Keystone XL oil, has stated that they're going to export it to nations overseas."

"Valero is one of the few refiners in the country," he said, "that gets its oil from America and sells its oil to Americans."

"Well, I can't tell you the history of Valero, but I can tell you they aren't selling that oil to America. The pipe won't do much to lower gas prices."

Reverend David, seeing that things were heating up, interrupted to say that we had to head back to his house because dinner was ready. Storms, who also seemed to want to avoid conflict, tried to steer the conversation down a more peaceful path.

But Bobby jumped in, pointing at my face again. "What do these protesters care about whether this pipe goes through this or that person's land?"

"Grubby-looking people," his mom chimed in, looking at me.

"Well, for them, it's not a local issue. It's a global one."

I was about to bring up global warming, which I knew would have enraged Bobby, but Reverend David got up and began to nudge us out of Bobby's house.

The next day, as we began our walk south again, I thought about all of the things I could have said to Bobby and how much more persuasive I could have been. I supposed it didn't matter, though; Bobby wasn't going to change his mind no matter how much evidence was put under his nose, as he'd never be convinced of something he didn't wish to believe. The battle over climate change, I thought, like the battle over civil rights, will not be won by convincing disbelievers of facts or appealing to their morality but by passing the torch of reason down to the generations to come, who will replace and laugh at us all.

19.

The Cop

February 8, 2013

←→

How would my journey end?

Perhaps it would end heroically. I'd imagined that after months of toil and deprivation I'd be on my last legs. Gaunt and haggard, starving and sun beaten, I'd stagger toward Port Arthur's Sabine-Neches Waterway, where I was determined to place my final footsteps. Just before reaching the water, I'd collapse to my knees, and drawing from the very last of my energy reserves, I'd crawl the last few feet to the finish line. Finally, with my last ounce of strength, I'd defiantly plop into the water, from which I'd be lifted out by a throng of admiring fans as if I were a a limp piece of meat.

But upon leaving Beaumont, Texas, on the morning of the last day of my trip, I was so well rested and well fed I could hardly zip up my pants. I'd spent the past two nights fattening up in a house on the northern edge of town, where I had stayed with a guy named Pete and his wife, Beth, who fed me as much gumbo and beer as I could handle. Pete and Beth had found my blog and offered their place to me, and I chose to extend my stay an extra night because another blog reader, Woody, offered to pick me up from Port Arthur on the afternoon of February 7.

In the morning, I filled up a small backpack with a bit of food and water, laced up my boots one last time, and left Pete and Beth's home just as the sun rose behind a bleak overcast sky. It would be a long day—twenty-six miles—and I had to finish by four p.m. so I could pick up a box of clean clothes and shaving clippers at the post office before it closed.

I walked along Eleventh Street through Beaumont's chain-store commercial district. I noticed, as I cruised through the city, that over the past five months I'd turned myself into a hiking machine. The soles of my feet were smooth and hard. My legs, accustomed to the daily motions of a long march, no longer felt sore. My shin had healed, my knees were tough, my back and shoulders sturdier than ever. My mind was no longer an assembly line or an art studio; it was a gentle breeze, at ease, peaceful, uncomplicated, perhaps even a little slower, a little simpler than it had been before. I had just walked across the country, and I knew I could keep going and walk across the world if I wanted to.

I took my first break in an empty parking lot. I was eating one of my last energy bars when a lady pulled up in her car to ask me if I was the guy who she'd seen standing on top of the overpass.

"No, I don't think that was me," I said.

"I thought you were going to jump," she said, dipping her hand into her pocket to offer me a handful of money.

I continued on down West Port Arthur Road, hiking next to white petroleum holding tanks in the shape of giant cat-food canisters that sat beside the overgrown grounds of Spindletop's Lucas Gusher (which, in 1901, triggered the oil boom in Texas). I walked alongside the occasional rusted pump jack slowly nodding its head like an old man falling asleep and waking up during church service.

As I approached the refineries, each mile greeted me with a new smell. After the first wave of your standard, and vaguely enjoyable, rotten-eggs stench, I was hit by the slightly more pleasant but more unsettling aroma of smoldering fireworks. Finally, the smell evolved into something more toxic, something more synthetic: a bubbling cauldron of chemicals, a bonfire put out by a gallon of Windex. My tongue began to tingle, so I tried my best not to swallow.

I was in Mordor, on the last leg of my journey, heading toward the summit of Mount Doom: the Valero refinery, with its billowing smokestacks and spouting towers of fire. Unpleasing to the eye and nose as it was, I was happy to be here. I was learning. I was stimulated. I was traveling. To get to the heart of America, we cannot simply walk its forests and fields; rather, we must cut through its industrial under-belly and pull out and examine its organs: its railways and refineries, its coal plants and pipelines. Its guts.

I felt a sense of acceptance looking at the litter, the pollution, the industrial wasteland. It wasn't that I'd come to accept these things as okay or that I'd become numb to them. But I was sick and tired of constantly feeling angry and powerless and frustrated. I came to ac-knowledge: This is how things are, this is the world we live in, and I can't wish or curse these things away. And I ought not restlessly long for what I wish the world would be but enjoy it for what it is, fight for what's right, and keep putting one foot in front of the other. And that's just what I did, kicking a cardboard box of Bud Light out of my path and stomping over an empty can of Dr Pepper.

I was done thinking we were on an irreversible path to a fiery apocalypse. Because here's the thing: We truly don't know what the future holds or how climate change will play out or whether we will, in fact, all die a cruel skin-melting death under a merciless sun. I don't question the science; I question our ability as humans to predict anything. There's a lot that can happen between now and doomsday. We're worried about a series of "positive feedbacks," in which one change in the environment can lead to another and another until the planet either turns into a smoldering Venus or a giant snowball. But there is such a thing as a "negative feedback," too. Kerry Emanuel, an MIT scientist and the author of *What We Know About Climate Change*, warns that we should be "wary of our own collective ignorance of how the climate system works. Perhaps negative-feedback mechanisms that we have not contemplated or have underestimated will kick in, sparing us debilitating consequences . . . Prediction beyond a certain time is impossible." This isn't an excuse to give up on conservation efforts because everything might turn out okay; it's a reason to keep working and caring and believing that our efforts matter. Perhaps it's best to believe, whether or not the end truly is coming, that the best of civilization will survive and our efforts will still be valued even if, regrettably, there is death and submerged islands and swamped coast-lines, too.

To give in to despair is to place too much faith in how much we know. Negative feedbacks, an enlightened and fed-up citizenry, a golden age of democracy, an ecoterrorism crusade, and, hell, maybe even help from aliens are all possibilities, if distant ones. Perhaps fortune will give us time. Maybe a few minicollapses will force us to turn more enthusiastically toward instilling a conservation ethic. For those who care about the species, the best of civilization and the earth, we thankfully have neither the knowledge of the future nor the ability to confidently predict it. Ignorance, the bane of climate-change action, weirdly, can be our salvation, too.

And as E. O. Wilson might say, let's not save the world for the sake of saving the world. Let's try to save it for the sake of saving ourselves. Our biophilia is about loving the earth, its life forms, its beauty, and perhaps even its future, and that means loving it whether the world will end tomorrow or in ten billion years. Do I say any of this with optimism, certainty, or a sense of empowerment? Nothing of the sort. But look into the darkness long enough and you might start to notice something sort of like hope.

I was approaching the Valero refinery. Pipes emerged from the ground like bamboo rods. Smokestacks puffed out white smoke. I was surrounded by an astonishingly complex network of pipes and steel and flaming towers and holding tanks. I couldn't begin to understand what each part did, how this whole place worked, or how much thought and labor and ingenuity went into building it.

I felt something close to what I had felt at the beginning of my trip nearly 136 days earlier when I flew over the tar sands of northern Alberta. There, I glided over muddied waste pits that looked like they had been carved out by life-ending meteors. I flew over eerie yellow sulfur pyramids, smoking refineries, and a horizon-to-horizon wasteland where fish once swam, moose once browsed, and natives once hunted. Yet above all of that devastation, I'd hardly felt a thing. I was more concerned about not dropping my camera out of the plane's window.

Looking at the tar sands and now this refinery, I felt something strange, and I felt guilty feeling it. I was *impressed*. I was impressed by its size and complexity, impressed by how many workers and how much labor had gone into creating this, impressed by how the human mind—or a collection of human minds—could build something so incredibly sophisticated. I was impressed, not because what we've done is good but because what we've done is amazing. As a member of this incredible species, I felt impressed, proud, and, most of all, hopeful. *If we can do this, what else can we do?*

"**H**ELLO!"

    I was startled by a loud robotic voice behind me. I jerked my head around to see a cop talking into the microphone in his car.

He got out, and said, "In Texas, you should walk against the traffic, on the other side of the road. You never know when a drunk driver will run off the road and hit you from behind.

"You weren't the guy taking photos of the refinery, were you?" he added.

"Yeah, that was me," I said, looking ahead to the Dr. Martin Luther King Jr. Memorial Bridge less than a mile ahead. I was eager to place my feet in the water beneath it to conclude my journey.

"They called up complaining," he said.

"Well, I won't be around long," I said. "I've been walking for 1,900 miles and 136 days. This is my last mile. I'm going to end my trip beneath the bridge over there."

He shook my hand and wished me luck. But less than a minute later, another police car, as well as a Valero security truck, had parked behind me with their lights flashing.

Oh, what now? I thought.

"Sir," one of the officers said. "I was telling my partner what you were doing, and she wanted a picture with you."

I gladly took pictures with the officers and continued on. Pete from Beaumont was taking photos of me up ahead, and Woody, also a professional photographer, was positioning himself ahead for shots.

When I got to Pete, who was standing by his car in front of the bridge, two more cops pulled up behind him and asked for his ID.

"The refinery is pissed," said the policewoman, exasperated.

"Don't take any more pictures of the refinery," said the policeman. "They don't like it."

It was four fifteen p.m., and I had to get to the post office before five p.m., so I was eager to get my feet in the water. There was a levee under the bridge surrounded by a fence and barbed wire, so if I wanted to get my feet in the water, I'd have to cross this quarter-mile-long, unusually steep, definitely sketchy shoulder-less bridge. Things began to feel a little chaotic. I wasn't sure if Pete was going to get arrested or a ticket, I was running out of time, and I had this last obstacle in front of me.

"I'm going to try to walk it," I told Pete, who was still being interrogated by the police. "If it's too dangerous, maybe I'll turn back."

I hopped onto the bridge and walked the narrow eighteen-inch-wide elevated concrete guard on the left side. I looked at my watch, and between the sense of urgency created by my logistical conundrum and the excitement of ending my journey, I took off on a sprint up the bridge. While running, I looked down on the elevated grassy levees, then the wide waterway, and finally the lush wetlands of Sabine Lake, which looked all the more pretty since I had just passed through Port Arthur's grim industrial district. I didn't care about preserving energy or being in pain tomorrow. This was the end, and I had the freedom to give it my all. So I ran, and I ran hard.

I left the bridge and, saturated in sweat, continued my jog on Pleasure Island, running toward a small mosquito-infested park where Woody and Pete (who didn't get arrested) were stationed with their cameras. I descended the muddy eroding bank, took off my boots, and sank my feet into the water of Sabine Lake, which empties into the Gulf of Mexico—the final step of the journey.

I had imagined this moment many times on my walk and I had already experienced the emotions that this moment might bring, so I didn't really need to experience them again. Each time I had imagined the end, I'd come close to tears thinking about all the people I'd met. My hitchhike drivers up to Canada, Harold and his giant Mormon family in Alberta, Ron and Eleanor in Saskatchewan, Patty and Lewis in Montana, Rick and Heidi in Nebraska, Harold and Maralee in Kansas, Dusty and Darcee in Oklahoma, Pete and Beth in Texas, and the hundreds of others, and I would feel this deep sorrowful love for my fellow man and this anachronistic but very real pride in being North American.

I thought about how the Thoreau in me was cynical, critical, misanthropic, at peace in the company of pine needles but crabby in the company of men. But also about how this trip had brought out the Whitman in me—a lover of all things, man and nature—and how sometimes I wanted to exuberantly catalogue all the professions of mankind in an epic poem, along with the clatter of our tools and the babble of our speech.

Oh, and the prairie. How I'd dream about the days spent walking over you, feeling the long feathery tails of your green grass waving against my legs, the cloud mountains sailing across the deep blue sky, the chatter of coyotes, the groans of cattle—and the stars, oh the stars. I'd feel melancholic thinking about you, about how I have you, yet don't have you at all. This life is so mortal, so finite, and I wished I could keep coming back to see you every year, forever, and savor your sights and these joys over and over again. Then you'd be mine. But I can't, and I'll have to be content with these memories and this sweet sadness—the sadness of having done but not having the lifetimes to do again.

After 146 days, 1,900 miles, eight states and provinces, three pairs of boots, and being taken care of by hundreds of strangers, I left the path of XL and got in Woody's car, where he helped me figure out how to get home.

20.

The Hiker

WASHINGTON, D.C.

2013–2014

← →

Woody and I drove to Washington, D.C., where we attended a big 35,000-person climate-change rally hosted by the likes of 350.org and the Sierra Club.

I couldn't help but feel a little shell-shocked. Just days earlier, I'd been walking across the country, often feeling very alone in my opposition to the Keystone XL, and suddenly there I was, surrounded by tens of thousands of people (many of whom were dressed as polar bears) hoisting signs that read KEYSTONE XL IS STEROIDS FOR CLIMATE CHANGE.

I was an insignificant atom among a shoulder-to-shoulder galaxy of bodies and signs and banners. It was all rather surreal, and as much as I agreed with the crowd's message, it was impossible for me to get swept up in the moblike fervor that had gripped other participants.

My ego was getting the best of me as I recognized that my days of having some sort of voice on this issue were almost over.

Hundreds of Nebraskans, opposed to the XL, came out for the rally, including Rick "the Governor" Hammond. They invited me to a pep rally at an Irish pub.

Upon entering, I was immediately given handshakes, pats on the back, and hugs from people I didn't even know. The Hammonds were there, as was Juanita, and hundreds from the Albion meeting. By the time I reached the other side of the bar, I had a giant mug of beer in each fist.

In the pub's basement, with two other outspoken landowners, I was ushered up on top of a booth table and the crowd called for a speech.

"I just walked 1,900 miles across North America," I called out. "I understand that there are a lot of landowners here who own land where the pipe is supposed to go through. First, I want to apologize for trespassing across your land. Second, I want to thank you for not shooting me." (Corny, I know, but it got a few laughs.)

"I don't want to waste your time. I'll just say that I went on this journey to learn about pipelines, but I learned more about the goodness of mankind. And that we all deserve better than this pipeline. No Keystone XL!"

The crowd was thoroughly soused, and the rowdy applause I received felt disproportionate to the quality of my speech. I was transported to the upstairs portion of the bar to give a second speech. I guzzled my third free beer and walked up to the booth with a cocky swagger. The booze and rowdy applause had gone to my head, and I had an untimely brain freeze in front of this newest throng and got down under a shower of tepid applause.

Eh. One for two, I thought.

. . .

flew back to Denver, got my van, and drove it to North Carolina, where I moved back in with my friend David at his hermitage in the woods of Stokes County. I resumed my routine of growing a garden, raising chickens, and attending monthly antifracking meetings with a local environmental group. My first book was published and I was invited on *The Tonight Show with Jay Leno*. But don't let me give the impression that my life was nothing but high excitement and uninterrupted productivity. I watched a lot of *Game of Thrones* in my underwear, struggled with the question of *What should I do next?* and dealt with some of the concerns of a young American male: *Should I upgrade to a Mac? Is that a lump on my testicle? Should I sign up for Obamacare? Should I start home brewing or am I having a thirty-year life crisis?*

It took my bruised hips—from the strain of my backpack—almost half a year to fully heal. Thanks to my hike, my little toe and shin splints give me the occasional spasm of pain to this day, but I think of them as well-earned scars I'm proud to bear.

My hike had received recognition in several small-town newspapers, a few local TV stations, and a couple of bigger media outlets such as the CBC, *Mother Jones*, and the *New York Times*. At most, the unusual nature of my trip helped bring more awareness of the XL to a few people who otherwise wouldn't have become acquainted with it. But the laying of the pipe in Oklahoma and Texas was never brought to a halt, the tar sands are bigger than ever, and the climate continues to change.

Truthfully, there's rarely a happy ending to a journey. Destinations are downers, and any step down from the height of existence will feel anticlimactic. But my hike has nicely settled into my memory as "the time I did that crazy thing and trespassed across the country." I think of all the people I met and the sights I saw, and, I feel as if I'd spent five months of my life as well as a human being might.

After my journey ended, President Obama, then in his second term of office, went on an unexpected environmental spree. Working around a recalcitrant Republican-led Congress, Obama secured a landmark emissions agreement with China and made a historic visit to the drowning villages of the Alaskan arctic, and the Environmental Protection Agency called for power plants to dramatically reduce CO_2 emissions. Up in Canada, the oil-crazed, tar sands–obsessed Harper government was toppled in the 2015 elections, making way for the environmental friendly Trudeau-led liberals. The wave of indignation behind the XL demonstrations and climate change rallies were being validated by sea changes in national policies and political landscapes.

And on November 6, 2015—after five years of demonstrations, court battles, and appeals to the president—Obama surprised the country by rejecting the northern portion of the Keystone XL.

The news made me think about how Nebraska's drinking water was safe from dirty oil spills. How Rick's family's farm wouldn't have a big pipe running through it. And about how the tar sands industry received a big blow to its plans. But I also knew that this was just one small victory in a war humanity will be fighting for a long time. A war where larger battles will need to be won. If I felt something less than jubilation, it wasn't because I didn't care anymore; it was because I now cared about something much bigger.

While we don't yet know the implications of its rejection, the fight over the XL triggered a new trend in pipeline opposition. By late 2015, pipelines with names like Northern Gateway, Sandpiper, Energy East, and Dakota Access were being passionately fought—fought not just by liberals and college students, but by a broadened, more diverse environmental movement, now including among its ranks farmers, ranchers, Native tribes, and salt-of-the-earth Great Plains landowners.

It seemed pipelines were destined to the outmoded fate of horse-drawn wood wagons and whaling ships sooner than imagined. The coal, gas, and oil industries were under siege like never before. Perhaps it's just a mirage on the horizon, but it appears we are moving—albeit at a steady crawl—toward a future with far fewer fossil fuels.

There's a saying on the plains that goes something like "Once you wear out a pair of boots, you won't want to leave." On my hike, I wore out three pairs of boots. I'd often find myself looking west to our great forgotten land, our Heartland of stars and skies and grass, where in the chorus of denial there are still calls for rebellion, where the cow roams and where the buffalo are coming back, where one of the great environmental fights of the twenty-first century took place.

A year later, I got in my van and sped west through Virginia, West Virginia, and Ohio. It broke down and died in Marshalltown, Iowa. I was stuck in the middle of nowhere with a pile of possessions, a dead van, and no place to go. I called my old hiking partner Rick Hammond, who, without hesitation, drove five hours one way to pick me up.

In a matter of hours, I'd crossed back onto the plains, left my gas guzzler behind me, put my past in the past, and found myself on America's original frontier.

I walked back out onto the prairie and trailed my fingers in the wavy grass, whose grainy tips felt like a trail of stardust.

I thought about how, when you spend months walking across the country, you're not just traveling over hills and grassland but over

Pleistocene glaciers, alongside Sioux horsemen, and within the Big Ag ranches and oil boomtowns of today. For the stationary person, time moves slowly if it moves at all. The stationary person has a keen eye for the present. Time is measured by a period of years: the growth of children, the lifetime of a roof, the passing of parents. And he thinks he is at the end point of a long story that has led up to that moment and that there isn't anything to add, as things will forever exist as they currently are. But the hiker sees something else. He sees the glaciers shaping the land, the stars wheeling overhead, the buffalo trails replaced with asphalt roads, the grass replaced with corn, and he recognizes that this moment is not the end but one blip of a billion beginnings. He not only walks the world but crisscrosses the paths of history.

The stationary person is vehemently defensive about conserving his way of life, as if protecting how things have always been is the noblest of virtues when, truly, our fossil-fuel-powered economy is but 150 years old. But any hiker knows that what can be done in 150 years can just as quickly become undone. And when I thought of climate change, I couldn't predict what the future had in store, but I felt an odd comfort in knowing that if the land, animals, and climate can change, so can we.

A pipeline is built to send a resource from a place that has a lot of it to a place that doesn't. But civilization won't collapse without new oil pipelines; it'll collapse without clean water, healthy soil, and a stable climate. What we ultimately need, it seems, cannot be delivered by a pipe.

Walk across America and see, within us all, the deep reservoirs of goodness, the wellsprings of love, our unthinking diligence, and our scientific genius, and you can't help but believe that—with nimble hands, inventive minds, compassionate souls, and, most of all, a good pair of feet—we can go far.

BIBLIOGRAPHY

Anderlik, John M., and Richard D. Cofer Jr. "Long-Term Trends in Rural Depopulation and Their Implications for Community Banks," *FDIC Quarterly* 8, no. 2 (2014): 44–59.

Anderson, Jerry L. "Britain's Right to Roam: Redefining the Landowner's Bundle of Sticks," *Georgetown International Environmental Law Review*, 19 (2007): 375–435.

Berry, Wendell. *The Art of the Commonplace*. Berkeley: Counterpoint, 2004.

Egan, Timothy. *The Worst Hard Time*. New York: Houghton Mifflin, 2006.

Emanuel, Kerry. *What We Know about Climate Change*. Cambridge: MIT Press, 2012.

Flores, Dan. *The Natural West*. Norman, Ok.: University of Oklahoma Press, 2003.

Fowler, Loretta. *The Columbia Guide to American Indians of the Great Plains*. New York: Columbia University Press, 2003.

Frank, Thomas. *What's the Matter with Kansas?* New York: Henry Holt, 2005.

Frazier, Ian. *Great Plains*. New York: Picador, 2001.

Hurt, Douglas. *Problems of Plenty*. Ann Arbor: University of Michigan: Ivan R. Dee, 2002.

Kaye, Frances M. *Goodlands*. Edmonton: AU Press, 2011.

Leopold, Aldo. *A Sand County Almanac*. Oxford: Random House, 1970.

Macfarlane, Robert. *The Old Ways*. New York: Viking, 2012.

Manning, Richard. *Rewilding the West*. Berkeley: University of California Press, 2009.

Martin, Paul Schultz. *Twilight of the Mammoths*. Berkeley: University of California Press, 2005.

McKibben, Bill. "Global Warming's Terrifying New Math." *Rolling Stone*, July 2012.

Mitchell, John Hanson. *Trespassing*. Darby, Pa.: Diane Publishing Company, 2000.

Nikiforuk, Andrew. *The Energy of Slaves*. Vancouver: Greystone Books, 2014.

———. *Tar Sands: Dirty Oil and the Future of a Continent*. Vancouver: Greystone Books, 2010.

Norgaard, Kari Marie. *Living in Denial*. Cambridge: MIT Press, 2011.

O'Brien, Dan. *Buffalo for the Broken Heart*. New York: Random House, 2007.

Owen, David. *The Conundrum*. New York: Riverhead Books, 2011.

Pipes, Richard. *Property and Freedom*. New York: Vintage, 1999.

Rosenberg, Norman J. *A Biomass Future for the North American Great Plains.* Netherlands: Springer, 2007.

Savage, Candace. *Prairie: A Natural History.* Vancouver: Greystone Books, 2004.

Slotkin, Richard. *Regeneration through Violence.* Norman, Ok.: University of Oklahoma Press, 2000.

Solnit, Rebecca. *Wanderlust.* New York: Penguin, 2001.

Stegner, Wallace. *Wolf Willow.* New York: Penguin, 2000.

West, Elliot. *The Way to the West.* Albuquerque: University of New Mexico Press, 1995.

Webb, Walter Prescott. *The Great Plains.* Lincoln: University of Nebraska Press, 1981.

Williams, Florence. "Plains Sense." *High Country News* (Paonia, CO), January 15, 2001.

Wilson, E.O. *Biophilia.* Cambridge: Harvard University Press, 2003.

———. *The Future of Life.* New York: Vintage, 2003.

Worster, Donald. *An Unsettled Country.* Albuquerque: University of New Mexico Press, 1994.

———. *Dust Bowl.* New York: Oxford University Press, 2004.

ACKNOWLEDGMENTS

First and foremost, I'd like to thank the Hammond and Harrington families of Nebraska for lending me space on their property to write this book. I owe a debt of gratitude to Josh Pruyn and Amelia Larsen for sparing their extra bedroom in Denver; Ron and Eleanor Caswell for hosting me not just once, but twice, on my travels through Saskatchewan; and Catherine Jourdan of Winston-Salem for giving me a place to stay as I perused the library shelves of Wake Forest University. Special thanks to David Dalton for his thoughtful edits and lovely home; Dean C. Smith, Storms Reback, Marianne Schubert, and Professor Jerry L. Anderson for help with research; and Rebecca Goodstein, Sarah Rice, Shannon Buckmaster, Jessica Blank, Rachel Bellavia, and Rebecca Biasi for their thoughtful critiques. Thanks to Cadence Cook for help with photo edits, and Amy and Peter Bernstein for their encouragement. And thanks to all the kind and generous folks along my route who fed, housed, and took care of me.

ABOUT THE AUTHOR

Ken Ilgunas has worked as an elementary school tutor, an Alaskan tour guide, and a backcountry ranger at the Gates of the Arctic National Park. He has a BA in history and English from SUNY Buffalo, and an MA in liberal studies from Duke University. He is the author of the travel memoir *Walden on Wheels* and currently lives on a farm in Nebraska.